# A Place That's
## *Warm*
### and
## *Beautiful*

A Journey to Faith

**Jane Ackerley**
**with**
**Marilyn Pincus**

ISBN 978-1-64079-210-4 (paperback)
ISBN 978-1-64079-211-1 (digital)

Christian Faith Publishing, Inc.
832 Park Avenue
Meadville, PA 16335
www.christianfaithpublishing.com

Printed in the United States of America

I dedicate this book to the four Js and all family and friends connected to them. I love you all and feel so blessed that you are part of my life.

# Acknowledgments

First, I thank God. I could never have done this book without the *faith* I have in the Lord and the power that he gives through the Holy Spirit.

I thank all the people who in some way contributed to my inspiration and knowledge in creating this book. I know who you are, and you do too. If you don't find your name in this acknowledgment portion of the book, it is only because space limitations make this impractical. Please know I feel blessed to have you in my life.

I gladly express my sincere gratitude to all those who provided support in reading, offered comments and prayer, or assisted toward the completion of this book. In particular, I would like to thank Marilyn Pincus for her collaboration in the editing, proofreading and designing, and offering clarity and insight that may not have otherwise occurred to me.

Above all, I thank my husband Julian and my daughter Jennifer and her husband Jesse, who supported and encouraged me during this process. I declare my love and gratitude for Joseph, my son, who helps to spiritually sustain me. I am grateful to them all for their patience with me as I worked to complete yet another goal, which without their love and support would not be possible.

My mom and dad, both deceased, helped to forge my personality; and they must share in taking credit for every objective I ever attain. This book, *A Place That's Warm and Beautiful*, is one of those objectives; and I acknowledge them here with love.

So many people reached out to us when our son Joseph passed away. I thank them again for the cards and letters and the meals and novenas they provided that helped to comfort us in our time of gut-wrenching grief. It is fitting that I do so here since this memoir revolves mightily around Joseph and his place in my life.

Thanks also belong to the many professionals, staff, and patients who have enriched my life along the way. This is particularly true of the psychiatrists with whom I have worked and grown through the years: Dr. Virgil Hancock, Dr. Wen Cai, and Dr. Marshall Jones.

And thanks belong to my many friends who provided a therapeutic environment for me when needed in the form of lunches, outings, walks, and talks. I feel compelled to name Nancy Day, who has spent countless hours walking and talking with me during more than thirty-five years of our friendship!

Last but not least, when I asked Msgr. Thomas Cahalane if he would write the foreword for my book, he did not demur even though demands on his time are unrelenting. For his time and consideration I am indebted, and this is true too for all those spiritual leaders who have prayed for our family over the years and helped to guide us.

*Gratias vobis ago* (I enact thanks to y'all).

# Contents

# Foreword

This memoir, by my good friend Jane Ackerley, is surely appropriately titled *A Place That's Warm and Beautiful*. It is transparently revealing and very autobiographical. In my ministerial experience as a priest, I have found again and again that Jesus drips off personal faith witness. The heart of Jane's sharing's in these pages is a rich personal testimonial in faith.

The memoir is the beautiful story of a soul nourished and sustained by God's presence through the Word and lifted on high through life's music. Jane's vivid recollections of her pilgrimage to the Holy Land translate into what is a common pilgrimage experience there and described by experts as the "fifth Gospel." Walking the footsteps of Jesus there and reflecting on his word spoken in particular places make the four Gospels come alive.

This memoir of warmth and beauty communicates a gentle, loving message from the wellsprings of a gentle and loving soul. From a faith perspective, it echoes into the larger reality of life the invitation of Jesus to his followers, "Take up your cross and follow me." Toward the end of the memoir, Jane observes, "The Lord knows the past, present, and future. You have to trust Him and take each step; one at a time." Jane, you did and you are continuing to take one step at a time as you proclaim through the words of the song by Casting Crowns:

> You never left my side
> And though my heart is torn
> I will praise you in this storm

May all who read this memoir be touched and enlightened by the singular spiritual intuitive gift of its author, who has shared so transparently with such a childlike gratitude, the story of a soul "that's warm and beautiful" in God.

Tomas O. Cathalain (Thomas O. Cahalane)

# Introduction

God told me to write a book, and it turns out to be this memoir, which is a story about my journey to faith. This is not the first time God has directed me to do something, and now I don't ask questions. I know if I don't act accordingly, he will pluck me off the current path and give me some other way to proceed. It's not always easy to do what he wants me to do, but I just do it. My faith is solid, and for the last six to eight months, I had this inclination to write. I went back to school and got a doctorate of nursing practice degree and wrote a forty-page paper that took an entire year to write. I got kudos for the paper, and that gives me confidence to write more, but where am I to find the hours to dedicate to the writing? It took me a long time to get to this place in my life, and I know, with every fiber of my being, that here is where I should be. *It is a place that is warm and beautiful.* I want to always be here and nowhere else. I know that when I die, this body will be done, but my soul and spirit will be released, and I will be with God forever and praising his name always, at peace and filled with love and praise for my God. Meanwhile, I am still on this earth—not a bad place to be when you look around at the beauty that God has put here: children, sunsets and sunrises, rainbows, birds, butterflies, and everything that surrounds me. All of it is special and created by God. I am also special, uniquely created. I wanted to love and serve God since I was a little kid. I had pitfalls, sins, and falling away from God at times; but I came back through the grace of God, and I sing his praises never to fall away again. It took me forty-nine years to get there!

## Why Now?

A short time ago, I underwent surgery, and I'm being treated for cancer. My mother recently passed away. My husband, Julian, lost his mother only a few weeks before my mother died. Julian's dad is devastated by the loss of his lifetime partner and needs our kindness more than ever. The piercing pain of our adult son's death by suicide does not abate. We watched our beautiful daughter Jennifer perform on stage last night and watched in awe. Two days ago while she was driving home from a rehearsal, there was a car accident that turned the front end of her car into mush. To tell you we had quite a scare is an understatement! I'm no longer a young woman, but as you just learned, I recently earned my doctorate degree. God directed me to do it, and at first I protested, "I can't do this." The work for the degree was immensely demanding. I had to shut out virtually everyone from my life while I studied. It has been years since I ate a leisurely lunch with friends or attended a family celebration from start to finish. After all this, shouldn't I take a time out? Apparently—not.

God wants me to write a book. *Write it now!*

We were attending a musical performance, and a woman approached me to say hello. She asked if she could give me her business card. She is a ghostwriter. *How cool is that?* I asked about her work, and she briefly explained she assists busy people who have something important to say in a book but don't have time to write it on their own. Sometimes, God uses things like this (i.e., a business card, an unexpected meeting, etc.) as *bread crumbs* to get me to follow a path. Remember the children's classic *Hansel and Gretel?* The children relied on bread crumbs on the ground to lead them to a place of safety. I kept the woman's business card, and a few months later, we began to collaborate on this memoir.

Soon after we started to work together, I asked her to come to church with me. It's important for her to know that God is *first and foremost* in my life.

I like to be in church on Sunday mornings, and Julian likes me to be there with him. Julian is the director of music at St. Francis De Sales Catholic Church in Tucson, Arizona, where Father Tamminga ministers to the congregation. I sing and play the guitar. Our family is also closely connected to Our Mother of Sorrows Catholic Church in Tucson where Msgr. Cahalane ministers to the congregation.

Julian is, and has been, the director of the Tucson Arizona Boys Chorus since 1980. Ours is a musical family! I daydream of playing rock and roll music, like Pat Benetar, but I rejoice in playing hymns. *How about becoming a Christian Rock Star! Why not?*

## A Place That's Warm and Beautiful

If you wonder at the title of this memoir, *A Place That's Warm and Beautiful*, it speaks to me of how I feel about my personal relationship with the Lord.

"We should include God in our daily lives. We should pray to Him, read His word, and meditate on verses in an effort to get to know Him better … We should take our requests to Him, asking in Jesus' name" (John 15:16). "Jesus is the one who loves us enough to give His life for us" (Romans 5:8); "He is the one who bridged the gap between us and God" (please see www.gotquestions.org/Printer/personal-relationship-God-PF.html).

There is a difference between being a religious person and having a relationship with God. *I didn't know this for a long time. As you read on, you'll discover how confronting this truth changed me completely.* I learned to have faith in God and to rest on my faith. I know the Lord has the best of things in mind for me, for each of us, and if we want to be in his *will* and do it his way, he will turn some pretty crummy things into something good for all those who love the Lord and are called according to his purpose. (I'm referring to Romans 8:28.) If you're willing to trust him, you just know that it's going to be okay. God will bless us. He is in control.

I write about deeply private matters in this book even though it's easier for me, and far more comfortable for those I care about, to leave these matters behind me. God did not tell me what to put into my book, but I know he wants the book to help others. It follows that, like it or not, some *secrets* had to be revealed. You'll find them in this tomb. At the same time, I'm going to step lightly on some information so as not to embarrass or upset anyone. This is my biggest challenge as I write this memoir. *I need to provide accurate information so the reader can appreciate the enormity of what I share while at the same time not reveal so much as to bring about ill will from any party.* To that end, I'll provide names of some places and people but not others.

## Spiritually Bankrupt

I have worked with people who are spiritually bereft. They've replaced belief in God with belief in drugs—thinking this will "fix" their problems. I'm here to stand as an example for them of how belief in God and Jesus is what people need for fulfillment in their lives. I know that true freedom is liberation from those outside forces that include illegal drugs, promiscuous sex, and alcohol and gambling addictions, which control lives and make people miserable. I am free. God is in control of my life. I have a healthy "addiction" or call it: an obsession, a hunger, a pressing urge, a rambunctious zeal that makes me sing out and share this "news" with others because it feels so good!

*I am free. God is in control of my life.*

Be aware: some web addresses you're directed to in this book were accessible at the time of this writing but may no longer be available to you. It's possible to locate additional information via the Internet. If, for example, you want to know more about "plasma donations," insert the words (*plasma donations*) into a search engine and see what you can find. Some popular search engines are google.com, yahoo.com, bing.com.

# *1*

## Early On

Back in Michigan, when I was seven years old, I wanted to go to church. My parents did not go to church except on rare occasions, but I wanted to go, and I did. The first time I attended, my parents gave me a coin to place in the collection plate and sent me off to a Baptist church, which was not far from our house.

In spite of my very early interest in attending church, I have only had a very personal relationship with the Lord for about twelve years. Before that, I was focused on things to do or not to do, such as attending church on Sundays, taking communion, and not eating meat on Fridays. *I didn't have a clue about what it meant to have a rich relationship with Jesus Christ.* And I attended several churches: a Lutheran church, a Methodist church, and went with a friend to a little Baptist church. I spent my sixteenth summer with my aunt and uncle in Alexandria, Virginia. They were Mormons, and that summer, I learned about the Mormon religion.

Julian is Catholic, and when we talked about getting married, he wanted me to become Catholic. I consented, and on our wedding day, I took my first communion. We agreed to bring up our children Catholic. Many years later when I asked Jesus Christ, "What am I?" I received the answer, "Born-again Christian." Since then if someone asks me about my religion, I am a born-again Christian in a Catholic church.

As a young girl, I took my parents to church. One of my first memories was when my dad went with me to a little Sunday school. It was so nice—so serene. Sometimes when I see the beautiful color green, I think of that church in Michigan surrounded by lush green trees and tall grasses. I remember just one time when my mom knelt down beside the bed and prayed with us. Otherwise, we never talked about religion at home. As I got older and could do things of my own volition, I went to church on Sundays, dragged my younger sisters with me, and got involved with the church choir. Julie, Joanna, Janice, and I received coins from our parents for the collection baskets. When we were all adults, Joanna told me that one time she and Janice took quarters or dimes or whatever they had been given and sneaked off to a Circle K store to buy candy. I didn't remember their escapade. But they do.

Once when Dad's sister, our aunt Jean, made cute little dresses with polka dots on the skirts for us; all of us went to church with her. Jean took us to a Catholic church. It was probably to show off the matching clothes on little girls who attracted admiring glances. I don't remember Jean encouraging us to attend church with her again. I was especially fond of Aunt Jean and would have been happy to attend church services with her again.

When I was in sixth grade, I decided to take my Bible to school. I remember looking at the first chapter of Genesis, but then I stopped. I did not understand what I was reading. When I was in eighth grade, I got my parents to take us to church so that we could all be baptized. By then we were living in Arizona. We went to the 22nd Street Baptist Church, and they had a little swimming pool above the altar. There was a huge window above it with a cross in the center. We all got totally dunked in the water. I remember my parents attended church with us one time after we were baptized, and that was the end of it.

We came to Arizona so my Dad could work here. He worked for Murray Bryant Chevrolet and later on worked for O'Reilly Chevrolet. He sold used cars and didn't make much money, but he had some wonderful hobbies. One of them was sewing, and he taught his daughters to sew. It was less costly to dress well if you designed and made your own clothes, and we did.

When we came to Tucson in 1962, I was looking for a church. I went to a little Bible chapel on the corner of Country Club and Grant. The pastor told the congregation that if we attended each Sunday for eight consecutive Sundays, we would get free pictures of Jesus. I wasn't going to miss getting a free picture of Jesus Christ! It is the Sallman Classic Christian Art Head of Christ. I coveted that picture, and it was on my bedroom wall for a long time. I'll never forget I was looking at that picture when I knelt to ask Jesus into my life. My sister, Joanna, who is younger than I, told me that I took her to church each of those Sundays; but she didn't get a picture. She got a bookmark and really wanted the picture. Even though this happened long before we were both grown and married, when I learned about it, I was able to find and order a copy of that picture for her. She was thrilled to receive it and told me when she saw what she had, she cried.

## A Spirited Child

You might say I was strong-willed, "uppity." My mother called me spirited and told my dad he should discipline but not break me. Was I rebelliously self-assertive, not inclined to be tractable or deferential? Perhaps. I was, however, an A student, so my parents didn't worry about my schooling. The one thing I know without question—I always felt as though I was different.

- *Uppity: (a dictionary definition) rebelliously self-assertive; not inclined to be tractable or deferential*

## Way Back When

I think of my childhood years at home and growing up. My parents supplied all our material needs. We always had food and a roof over our heads. There was something special about the way we sisters all had names beginning with the letter *J*. My parents liked those names. One of the names came from my mom's friend Joanna. They really liked that name and thought my name, Jane, is nice. It too was the name of a friend. They like the name Janice and Julie, too. It was as simple as that.

With all that was good and for which I was grateful, there were times when voices were raised inside our house and serenity was nowhere to be found. My parents were not perfect, but they were dear to me.

My parents didn't go to church or give us any instruction about the Lord. They did take us to get baptized after I got involved at 22nd Street Baptist Church and told them how important I thought that was. I must have been about twelve years old at the time. They did not object to my church attendance, and they always made sure I had coins to contribute to the collection plate.

My mom was a foster child, and in every sense of the word, she was a survivor. I loved her very much!

## Her Last Nine Years

Mom lived at Julie's house for nine years. My sisters and I had lots of contact with one another during that time. When Mom was ailing, we set up taking-care-of-needs shifts and helped out financially. My mom was the magnet that drew us together. Now that she is gone, I wonder if we will move into our own little worlds. The answer is we have made a point of getting together.

# 2

## Music Is Woven into the Fabric of My Life

*To stop the flow of music would be like the stop-
ping of time itself, incredible and inconceivable.*
—Aaron Copland, an American composer,
conductor, 1900-1990

Where to begin? For me music is everywhere. *Sometimes I think in
music!* I'll begin by telling you that my husband-to-be and I met
in high school, and we sang in our high school's choir;—an elite
choir known as the Jubileers. Music has taken us to thirty-two
countries.

*How's that for a place to begin?*

My husband, Dr. Julian Ackerley, has been the director of the
Tucson Arizona Boys Chorus since 1980. He received his Doctor
of Musical Arts degree from the University of Arizona with special
emphasis in music education and vocal and choral directing. Julian
has held this position for over three decades. We travel with the boys
in the chorus to perform at international festivals in China, Mexico,
South America, and Europe. We have seen hundreds of young boys
grow to be young men and leave us, and we have welcomed other
young boys into the chorus and watched them grow. I have served as
the registered nurse responsible for medical needs of choir members
and staff on domestic and international tours.

## A God Song

Many of the songs the Boys Chorus performs are what I call *God songs*. You may know them as liturgical music. Often when I arrive at the psychiatric health facility where I work as a psychiatric nurse practitioner, I'm humming a God song. I may sing it on my way down the hall when I walk to my office, and by the time I arrive, I'm serene and focused on what I'm doing. I have been melodically reminded that God has a hold on me. I praise him and praise him. How great our joy!

I started listening to God and turned my will and my life over to him. That is when I went back to school after fifteen years in order to be a nurse practitioner. God was urging me to do it, and so I did!

Returning to school after almost fifteen years since earning my master of science in psychiatric mental health nursing took unwavering determination and hard work. I attended the University of Arizona, and the initial work started before classes began. I had to take a leave of absence from my job to work toward my degree, and I had to learn how to use a computer. I wasn't even proficient with the keyboard. I had to learn how to navigate the Internet and become familiar with computer jargons (e.g., mouse, server, cursor, backup, boot, virus, login, icons, default)! On August 26, 2005, I wrote a note in my diary. *My computer skills are getting better! I now know how to put four PowerPoint slides on one page!* That may sound impressive, but I had a long way to go. During that time, one song in particular helped me to relax and feel good. It was a song about getting out of the boat … taking a leap of faith. You may know it, "Voice of Truth." The musical group Casting Crowns performs it, and here are some of the lyrics:

Oh what I would do to have
the kind of faith it takes to climb out of this boat I'm in
Onto the crashing waves

You can find the entire song—both the lyrics and music—on YouTube. Ask for "Voice of Truth," and you'll find many choices. You can also contact www.amazon.com to purchase this music or inquire at local stores where music is sold. You may enjoy this song as much as I do.

## You Can Be Anywhere

You've got to read God's words to know how God thinks. The manner in which God interacts with people is revealed through Scripture—the written Word, the Christian Bible, the Old and New Testaments. These were written thousands of years ago, but the Bible remains true today. You've got to focus on God and his words. It takes time. I make time for God.

Dr. Charles Stanley is the founder of In Touch Ministries, and his spoken words are heard by millions of people all over the world. I listen to him on audiotapes and live on the radio as often as possible. I read his books. I started listening to Charles Stanley in 2002. It was the beginning of my Bible study. He tells us he feels God's presence when he shaves and tells us he weeps like a baby. Each morning when I drive to work, I listen to Charles Stanley or R. B. Thieme, who is also a dynamic speaker, author, and Christian leader. Maybe that helps to explain why I feel God's presence when I'm in my car. The feeling is powerful. I can understand why it moves Charles Stanley to tears. It's sort of like he moves me into a different dimension. I'm attentive to my driving skills, but everything else is absent from me except a profound sense of peace and security. All that matters is him with me. ("A peace that surpasses all understanding," Philippians 4:7, this Bible verse multiplied by a thousand.) The sense of him there brings me to tears.

## Music Goes Hand in Hand with Worship

Did you ever notice how music is intertwined with spoken "instruction" when you listen to spiritual leaders? I never attended a church service that did not include song.

Psalm 150:1-6 (*English Standard Version*), "Let Everything Praise the LORD," tells us to

Praise the LORD!
Praise God in his sanctuary;
Praise Him in his mighty heavens!
Praise Him for his mighty deeds;
Praise Him according to his excellent greatness!
Praise Him with trumpet sound;
Praise Him with lute and harp!
Praise Him with tambourine and dance;
Praise Him with strings and pipe!
Praise Him with sounding cymbals;
Praise Him with loud clashing cymbals!
Let everything that has breath praise the LORD!
Praise the LORD!

I questioned myself about whether my devotion to Dr. Stanley's words "fit" in this chapter, "Music Is Woven into the Fabric of My Life." After all, Charles Stanley isn't singing; he is speaking. After giving this considerable thought, I decided his words act like music. When I am in fellowship with God and being filled with the Holy Spirit, I am seeing and hearing with the eyes of my soul. I have enormous regard for Dr. Stanley. Dr. Stanley was scheduled to take a trip to Jerusalem with many of his admirers, and Julian had arranged for us to go on that trip. My husband knew it would be a trip I would remember forever, and it was his graduation gift for me. Of course, I was eager to meet Charles Stanley, and when word came that he was not able to join us, it was a major disappointment. I repeat—a major disappointment. I was reminded, however, about the amazing trip ahead and the fact that we were going to be on ground where Jesus had walked and were going to see the land and waters and mountains Jesus had seen. I came to the conclusion the trip was about Jesus and not Charles Stanley. "And leaving the city Nazareth, he came and dwelt in Capharnaum on the sea coast …" (Matt. 4:13). The trip was all I had anticipated and more. (Thank you, Julian!)

The following is a simple copy of notes I made on my cell phone at that time: "Trip to Israel September 2-12, 2014. We saw Mt. Carmel, went to Nazareth, and saw a replica of the village in the time of Jesus. We went to Tiberias and Tel Dan, where we saw three-thousand-year-old ruins mentioned in Bible stories. It makes the Bible really come alive. We took a boat ride on the Sea of Galilee and sang Christian and Israeli songs on the way. It was an amazing experience.

Julian and I were baptized in the Jordan River with the little fish nibbling at our feet. We went to Jericho and ate a meal in an Arab restaurant. Then we went to the steps of the temple and had a service complete with a choir. It was a fabulous experience.

Today we went to the Western Wall and added our prayers to God. We saw many places where Jesus walked, preached, and was held captive in the pit; here it is so very meaningful it's hard to put it all into words. More in Jerusalem. Took the path of Christ. Walked down Via Delorosa. Saw the sight(s) where Christ was buried and resurrected.

Saw where the Dead Sea scrolls were buried in the caves. Went to Masada to see the last holdout of the Jews. They all died by suicide in the end so the Romans would not take them. We swam in the Dead Sea. No need to swim, because it was so buoyant. Last day spent time at the tomb. Our faith rests on the fact that Jesus is risen. Thank you, Lord, for this opportunity to learn and to grow.

God continues to speak to my spirit through his Word. It was not too long ago that I understood that I would be returning to Israel. I have no idea when or why, but it appears to be a part of God's plan.

## My Sister's Astonishing Car

In order to listen to R. B. Thieme Bible studies, I need to use an MP3 player.

I didn't always own an MP3 and didn't even know exactly what it was.

It turns out there was a player in my sister's Yaris. Not too long ago, she wanted to sell her car as quickly as possible, and I told her I would buy it. We sold my Lexus, although until the papers were signed, everyone kept asking me, "Are you sure you want to do this?" The Lexus is a remarkable vehicle. At the same time, the Yaris gets me everywhere I want to go, and my fuel costs have dropped dramatically, but most notably, an MP3 player is in the Yaris. My sister never mentioned the MP3 player, and, at first, I didn't notice it. I was thrilled to discover it because now I can hear all the audio sermons I want to hear while I drive. Could it have been a coincidence that the MP3 player was in that car? I say *no*. The Lord looks out for me. He does this with the little things as well as the big things. *God is awesome!*

*I praise you for what and who you are. I dance and move with joy when I think of the life and energy that you have given me. I thank you for your love and relationship with me, a special child of God, my father. To make the mistakes I have made and to be forgiven by you is humbling. Thank you for the consequences of my actions that have taught me and made me grow in character and in strength with you.* (I wrote this in my personal prayer journal at the beginning of 2004. How the years have dashed forward, and it's comforting to know; the praises I sang are as vibrant as ever!)

I have incorporated *a number of* problem solving devices into my new way of thinking. They come directly from R. B. Thieme, Jr., Bible Ministries *(from his teachings on Spiritual Dynamics and the Faith-Rest Life)*. All of the materials are free. "How ridiculous it is to collect Bible doctrine in your soul and not apply it to your circumstances. You learn doctrine to use doctrine." That admonition resonated with me! *Eventually, the way that we choose to live will have the ultimate consequence. People have free choice! The question comes down to "What do you think of Christ?" (Matthew 22:42). Salvation comes by grace alone, through faith alone, in Christ alone. Believe in the Lord Jesus and you will be saved (Acts 16:31). I'm going to paraphrase several of Thieme's concepts* here:

1) **Rebound**. One of the mysteries in the Christian life is the meaning and method of attaining spirituality, the absolute status of fellowship with God. It is a system of privacy and freedom that depends on God's grace and not on remorse, guilt or pious living. *Rebound means to confess sin privately to God to stay in fellowship with Him and then keep moving ahead! God is faithful to forgive us when we recognize and are accountable to Him the wrongs that we think, do, or say.* You can learn the easy to understand route that brings you here (1John 1:9) and why it is important (Ps. 32:3-4).
   (If you want details; refer to Thieme's Series # 376, Spiritual Dynamics, lessons 83-90, 136-140, Ten Problem Solving devices). http://rbthieme.org/tenproblemsolvingdevices. html).

2) **Be filled with the Holy Spirit**. This is one sure way to stand strong against sin. The Holy Spirit is in me. I need to maintain fellowship with God by confessing sins as they come up *(once again 1John 1:9).* Then He empowers me to reject the sin nature's control of my life. "Every Church Age believer has the privilege and opportunity of being controlled by God the Holy Spirit."

3) **Remember my faith rests on the Lord**. When problems arise I shall hang fast to God's promises. His promises become more real than emotions, circumstances or problems. *As a believer I have trusted Him for the big one: eternal salvation! Now I need to trust Him in my temporal relationship with Him for the day to day problems and crises that life*

*will inevitably throw my way. God wants us to do one thing, TRUST HIM. Believe His word, mix the promises of God with faith then wait for God to graciously meet that problem. The word wait in the Bible always means faith. Not for seconds or minutes but to keep on trusting God.*

(I am conversant with R.B. Thieme's Series No. 376, Spiritual Dynamics, lessons 99-208. I gladly refer you to R.B. Thieme, Jr. where you can obtain details.)

4) **Grace Orientation**. Arrogance creates problems but humility solves problems. At all times and in all situations resist the inclination to boast. Let others sing your praises, if they will. You and I are well served by learning humility. *God offers gracious provisions if we learn to trust and lean on Him. God is telling us He has wonderful things for us if we will just stand still and receive them (Heb. 4:3). Trying to find happiness under our own power rejects what God has provided for us.*

5) **Doctrinal Orientation.** Learn to think with the mind of Christ. I think about that. I think hard. Allow the Holy Spirit to work in me and through me. You can "think with the mind of Christ" if you are steeped in his teachings and make good decisions from a position *of His strength. He gives strength to the weary means that He exchanges our strength for His (Isa. 40:29). It doesn't get any better than that! Study God's Word and then put it into action with faith. Know the promises and claim them.*

6) **I know God has plans for me**. I need to recognize that I have personal potential in the plan of God. A sense of spiritual destiny will give me confidence to live in the light of an eternally secure future. Adversity fades compared to the spiritual self-esteem that comes from a limitless relationship with the Lord. *I need to believe the Word, lean on God and*

*stop depending on myself. His love never fails no matter how bad or how tough things get (Isa. 26:3-4). When I depend on Him then God is glorified, the Son is pleased and my life is changed for the better.*

7) **The Lord's love for me is unconditional**. This means I can be joyful. God has an unconditional love for *me* no matter what mistakes I make. The absolute confidence in His divine ability to care for me "supports and sustains momentum for problem solving and courage in the face of adversity." *God is pure righteousness and never changes (Heb. 13:8). Our spiritual life starts with a slender cord of faith with the promise of salvation and then grows by relying on God's promises and then more promises. Eventually that cord is strengthened through trust and dependence on the Lord.*

(Series No. 376, Spiritual Dynamics, lessons 514-517.)

8) **I can have an impersonal love for everyone through the eyes of the Holy Spirit**. This means everyone! Yes even people who are obnoxious or evil must be included if I'm to imitate the Lord. I can learn to exhibit virtue and love toward others and reserve the tranquility in my own soul. *But the fruit of the spirit is love, joy, peace, forbearance, kindness, goodness, faithfulness, gentleness, and self-control (Gal. 5:22-23). By maintaining fellowship with God (through rebound) and filling my soul with help from the Holy Spirit (John 14:26), these characteristics within me have an opportunity to shine and to have an unconditional regard towards all.*

9) **I have an attitude of gratitude**! Nothing less is acceptable. Give thanks to God through the good times and the bad. "When your spiritual life takes precedence over circumstances, you carry God's happiness with you as a constant companion." *The joy of the Lord comes from knowing Bible*

*doctrine in your soul and applying it to everyday situations (Ps. 100:5). God has provided a perfect, permanent happiness that does not rely on any human factor. The secret is "rest" in Him, which is faith, rather than trying to live life through the energy of the flesh.*

10) **I have found my role model and it is Jesus Christ**. The Holy Spirit living in me can live out this role as long as I am in fellowship with God. Purify me so that the Holy Spirit can be filled. My attitude can reflect Christ's perspective through occupation with Him. *Rather than a phony facade of hypocrisy or religiosity I can be a relaxed and stabilized individual by depending on God's Word. I can exchange my strength for His by simply trusting Him, and never by my own works (Eph. 2:9).*

## Sunday Travels

Wouldn't you know it, from 10:00 a.m. until 10:30 a.m., when I drive to church on Sundays, Rick Hughes is on the radio? His ministry is enlightening. It permits me to tune in to more of the nuts and bolts of the faith, and I wrote to him to ask if he could give me more information about his ministry and suggest a church in Tucson I could visit where I would hear more about the truth regarding the Bible. He sent books but did not have a church to recommend. "The Rick Hughes Evangelistic Ministries, Inc. was founded for the purpose of communicating the Word of God to students and administrators in private schools and churches across the United States" (www.goodreads.com/author/show/3082318.Rick_Hughes). It's a nondenominational ministry, and material isn't sold. This is how I learned about R. B. Thieme and exegesis. Exegesis refers to finding the truth by examining the original words in the context in which they were written. Apparently, the English translation has really taken away some of the true meaning of the original texts of the Bible written in Hebrew and Greek.

I read the books and read them again. I think the Holy Spirit points out something different each time I read. That especially happens with the Bible.

## Guitar and Piano

I don't watch television. I prefer to use that time to play my piano.

I always want to keep learning. I don't like crossword puzzles, and so I thought piano playing would keep my brain active. I took up the guitar again at age forty-eight. The first time I played, I was twelve and thirteen years old. My parents paid for one year of guitar lessons. I went with my friend Eleanor, who played guitar too, and we would play Beatle songs together, and that was fun. Once those years passed, I didn't pick up the guitar again until I was forty-eight years old. I had to build up those calluses on my fingers one more time. When I came back to it, I remembered the chords. Now I have an opportunity to play every Sunday at church. I had to give up piano lessons when I was working for my doctoral degree. I told my mom, "I'm going to use my piano brain to put toward a doctorate." She said, "You'll do it, Jane. Everything you go for, you always accomplish." Now I'm taking lessons again. It would be terrific to play the piano at church. *First things first, learn how to play the piano well!*

## Jennifer, on Stage

Jennifer loves theatre and is a talented performer. She studied in New York City. She earned her undergraduate degree and master's degree in business and is well prepared to step into a business career should she eventually choose to do so. I prayed that she would get a job in the theatre when she finished her studies in New York, and she got a one-year contract with the Great American Playhouse.

A visitor to our home in the early morning may wonder what it is she hears. If she is listening to a range of pleasing tones filling the air and our daughter Jennifer is staying with us, then what she hears is Jennifer's beautiful trained voice practicing vocal scales. When Jennifer steps into the room to say hello, the visitor realizes that not only is Jennifer's voice lovely, so is Jennifer. She moves with an easy grace and looks as though she belongs on stage. Fact is, she is on stage!

Jennifer is living with us while she is performing locally. Her husband, Jesse Lawrence, was staying at our house too until he could no longer delay returning to their home in Vermont. Jesse was here when Jennifer was in the car accident that badly battered the front end of her car. He is a quiet man, but we listen attentively when he shares his insights. When he and I drove to the scene of the accident, his strong and calming presence was especially welcome. Jesse rode in the ambulance with Jennifer when she was taken to the hospital. I stayed on-site long enough to check on the condition of others who were involved. It appeared that injuries were minor. God's grace helped us through that one! Jennifer and Jesse were able to afford that car, thanks to sister-in-law Heidi Ackerley, who works at Jim Click Ford. That car was instrumental in saving Jennifer's life when all the air bags deployed, keeping the driver's compartment intact when the front of the car crumpled like an accordion. *It's a God thing!*

## Great American Playhouse

Jennifer is performing on stage at the Great American Playhouse on Oracle Road in Oro Valley, Arizona, about twenty minutes away from our home. Naturally, Julian and I attend performances, and I feel pure joy when I listen to our daughter sing and watch her dance and move about the stage.

Jeanne Eagels was a talented and successful actress—a star of silent films and early "talkies," and she was related to the Ackerley family. She was my father's-in-law aunt, which means she was a great aunt to Julian. She went on to work on stage in America and abroad and became a well-known winner of Hollywood awards. I could write pages and pages about her career, but suffice it to say she has a solid place on the Ackerley Family Tree, and you may agree this should serve as a source of satisfaction and encouragement for any Ackerley who wants a showbiz career.

## Music at Bar Mitzvahs

I smile when I remember that Julian and I had a band.

The band started when we were in high school. Some friends from the high school choir joined us. The band's name, Paradox, was actually a vocabulary word one of the band members had to memorize. He suggested it, and it stuck. So we were known as Paradox. Other musicians joined us when we attended college. We were still band members when we were in our early twenties and married. But when our first child was due, Julian and I retired from the band.

We played music at weddings and bar mitzvahs. We learned how to play and sing "Hava Nagila" in the Hebrew language since it is frequently performed at Jewish celebrations. We supplemented our income with our music engagements.

## A Little like Music

I have been saying a little prayer each morning for twenty years. It is the Jabez prayer, and mention of it belongs in this book. I decided to tell of it right here in this chapter, "Music Is Woven into the Fabric of My Life."

I don't sing this prayer, but I could. It has a lot in common with music: passion, soft and loud tones, and a commanding presence; and it reaches a crescendo.

> *Here is my version of the Jabez Prayer:*
> *Bless me, bless me, bless me, Lord.*
> *Increase my responsibility, my influence for you, with your*
> *hand on me of course.*

*Keep me from temptation, anger, and evil and keep those things far, far away from me.*

I also put on my spiritual armor daily (Eph. 6:11-13, NIV). There is (1) the Belt of Truth, (2) the Breastplate of Righteousness, (3) the Sandals of Peace, and more. This is a mental exercise that prepares an individual to move into the day knowing how to fight evil. God gives us detailed instructions.

## You Can Do It Too

There is another Casting Crowns song that helped to motivate me in addition to their song "Voice of Truth." This next song is "Praise You in This Storm."

When the Lord told me to go back to school to study for my postmaster's nurse practitioner's certification, I was short on courage, and this song helped to get me through tough times. Casting Crowns sang, and I listened over and over to giving praise to God through the most difficult times and trusting in his truth.

The Lord knows the past, present, and future. You have to trust him and take each step—one at a time. I did, and the more I did, my faith would grow, and by the time I got into a doctoral program, my attitude was … *Okay, whatever you want, I will do.* I'm not going to worry about this or that. I'm not going to worry about where money to pay for this education comes from. I'm not going to worry about how to get to Texas to give my dissertation. God has got the whole thing figured out. He does provide. He will provide. And I learned he did it. It was scary to go back to school for these advanced degrees, especially at my age; still I stepped out of the boat and wavered a few times, *Oh no, the waves are too high. The wind is too strong. This will never happen.* But deep down, I kept believing and working, and it happened!

## No Easy Way to Tell You

I can't find a comfortable way to tell you about some of those desperately unhappy times in my life. I can't find a sensible place to insert these descriptions into my book. So I'm going to stop everything and do it now. I'm telling the story my way—not wishing to put blame anywhere or on anyone but myself. I am leaving out "chunks" of information because you don't have a need to know. But *you do have a need to know things were desperate for me*; and my health, happiness, and well-being were seriously in jeopardy. Allow me please to demonstrate:

*A Perfect Storm*

*Perfect Storm* describes an event where a rare combination of circumstances will aggravate a situation drastically. This "confluence" resulted in one particular event of enormous consequences (http://en.wikipedia.org/wiki/Perfect_storm).

*I placed so many people who were close to me (e.g., family, friends, and colleagues) on pedestals. I thought of them as perfect. I treated each one as ideal. God never told us to put our trust in people but to put our trust in him. One by one, for various reasons, the people toppled down from those heights. When that happened I concluded "I could not count on anyone."* I was pulled by angry feelings and despair over the actions of others. I love them, and they may love me, but that is different. I can't fully count on them. That realization hurt so much. I felt stranded, alone—desperately alone. And I was frightened. *I didn't yet have a relationship with the Lord.* I had religion but not a relationship. It might have helped if long ago I woke up to the fact that having a relaxed mental attitude could have helped me let it go. But letting the "old sin nature" control me instead of being controlled by the Holy Spirit led me to making poor choices and dealing with consequences that last a lifetime. I was not filling myself with God's truth, and so my spirit was bankrupt. I was a Christian, but my spirit was full of scar tissue, and I was living out of my old sin nature. (Sin nature refers to man's natural inclination to sin.)

*I didn't know this!*

*The burden was enormous, and ultimately, I made some seriously wrong choices and was hospitalized.*

My behavior with unsanctioned drugs—even though it was for a brief period of time, a long time ago, and even though I was in pain and searching for help (not trying to be a party girl!)—showed me that I could not depend on myself. After that episode, just a short three months, I was hospitalized in 1986 when Jennifer was three years old. In 1974, I had earned my nursing degree. Now I was working on getting my masters in psychiatry.

I attended a convention in Phoenix where famous psychiatrists and researchers were speakers. I didn't enjoy the conference. I was *spaced-out.* I had a friend drive me home because I wasn't able to drive, and I arrived home sick—sick and psychotic. Jennifer came to the door and took me by the hand and led me to the Christmas tree. Julian and the children had decorated it that weekend while I was away. She was so proud. I was so compromised in my mind I could hardly see the beautiful white lights. I asked my husband to take me to the emergency room. He did, and after that, I got a little better. It wasn't until later that I had to be admitted to the hospital. Joseph and Jennifer came to the hospital to visit me at that time, and I remember being so happy that I could see them. They were quite young, and I thought when they get older, I don't want people to say, "Your mom used some substances she should not have used," but because of that experience, my life got better. I learned some very hard lessons. I didn't want them to think you could do those things and be okay. I was sent home on medication and got better. I told them both much, much later. I remember walking down a street with Jennifer and telling her. (*And one Christmas when Jennifer was thirty years old, I told her about that incident when I came home so spaced-out and she wanted to show the Christmas tree to me and I didn't appreciate it. She didn't remember that, but I said, "Let's do it now, Jennifer. We held hands and walked to the Christmas tree, and together, we admired all the lights.)* The smells and sounds of that walk are fresh in my mind. It was awful to have to tell her, but she loves her mom, and she knows I'm a human being and I come complete with human frailties.

All of our neighbors knew I had been hospitalized. They were nice enough people and nice to my children, but after that first episode, several people displayed an aversion to me. Julian didn't want to talk about my failings, and when a woman from across the street had questions and was talking about me to neighbors, he telephoned her and said he didn't want people gossiping about his wife, and he told her to stop. So we didn't talk about it. Again, I was on my own. At one point, Julian was out of town, and I got so sick. [I had stopped taking my medicine (i.e., lithium, which helped to keep my mood stable). I hadn't used any prohibited substances for many months and vowed never to use any kind of substance again, including alcohol. And yet the drugs had altered my thinking, and I became manic.] I couldn't stay by myself. I couldn't take care of the children. I stayed with Julian's parents while he was gone. I ended up in the hospital again—for a second time. I remember Msgr. Cahalane coming to visit me at the psychiatric hospital. He is a larger than life, faith-filled man, sensitive and caring. In his charming Irish brogue, he said, "Janie, you've got wild white horses driving you forward. Pull back on the reigns, and slow down!" His prayers were always comforting, but I just remember the wild white horses; it set up a vivid picture in my mind. It is exhausting to go to the hospital to deal with this kind of sickness, and when I returned home, I had to sleep more than usual, and I was on medication, which caused drowsiness. Jennifer and I were in the house together, and Joe was at school, and my eyes were closing. I asked God to just take care of Jennifer so I could close my eyes. I lay down on the couch, and I know that's horrible because she is only three years old, but I asked God to watch her, and I slept for about twenty minutes. When I woke and opened my eyes, she was standing there. I thanked the Lord for taking care of her. I still did not have a close relationship with the Lord at that time. I prayed to God based upon what I had seen and heard in church. *I had religion but not a relationship.*

Now my relationship with God is firm and unshakeable. The only one I can depend upon at all times is God. When you have him to hold onto and you've got your thinking straight about all the doctrine that's in the Bible to help you and the seven thousand-plus promises from God that are there to help you, that can keep you on track, and you don't have to fall apart and compromise your dignity and well-being.

And, yes, I did compromise myself, but I'm not going to fully elaborate on that except to say you may not be familiar with the term *manic*. Check your dictionary if you need to, but I will tell you the synonyms for the word *manic* are *frenzied*, *agitated*, and *frantic*. Picture me on the way to the emergency room with the car windows rolled down and me loudly crying out, "Go, God, go." It's like "Go, Dog, go," which is the title of the little book I used to read to my children. My kids were small at the time, and I was starting to get God into my life. So I was yelling that all the way down the street, and all the neighbors knew that Jane *is in trouble*. It was not a pretty picture, and, yes, it was demeaning, undignified, debasing, humiliating.

## More than One Way to Proceed

One woman of my acquaintance was not a regular church-goer, but when her husband left her and their three young children, she picked up the phone and started calling leaders of neighborhood churches. (Why didn't I turn to my spiritual leader when I felt hopeless? Without my breakdown, how-ever, I'm convinced I would not have been ready to engage in this precious relationship with the Lord that changed me for-ever.) In short order, this woman established a small network of people who were getting to know her and vice versa, and they were willing to help her. She didn't go to the street corner to find someone selling mind-altering substances, which, as it turns out, was very easy to find and to buy. She reached out for help in a healthy, productive way.

I can say, with complete candor, I have been on both sides of the mental health challenge. I've been broken and empty and know how that feels—down to the loss of every shred of per-sonal dignity. In one moment, I'm a highly valued and respected member of society, and the next moment that's all gone. *Poof.* The real Jane disappeared. She was so out of control. She had to be restrained and forcibly placed in a room that contained nothing—no stimuli. When I was released on medication and returned home, some people who knew of my collapse were des-perate to avoid me. It was all I could do to hold onto a smidgen of myself with the dysregulation of neurotransmitters in prog-ress within my brain. (*For your information*, neurotransmitters are chemicals released from nerve cells in the brain that transmit information to other cells known as receptors. Many psychiat-ric disorders are believed to be partly the result of abnormalities related to neurotransmitters and receptors in the brain. You can find this definition on the Internet.) My troubles were the result of a physiological phenomenon that was exacerbated by the use of mind-altering drugs and a deficiency in my relationship with God. I, however, must accept full responsibility for actions that were responsible for setting disastrous consequences in motion. Still, mental illness is not born of a personal desire to implode or explode, and yet you are faulted by those who don't have any understanding of the sickness or any compassion or kindness to give when it is needed most. So I have walked in the shoes of the mentally ill, and I have comforted and treated the mentally ill too. I studied long and hard to learn and earn my various degrees and certification and the terminal one, my doctorate. I've been hired by and worked with prominent physicians and experts in my chosen field and researchers who are always searching for better answers. I have their trust, and this I know full well from the assignments and praise I received. (One medical director, Dr. Don McDaniels, said such a nice thing to me in front of staff. He was talking about person-centered therapy and how we need to treat our patients with respect and compassion. He said, "Jane"—right in front of everyone—"the reason people keep coming back to see you is you care about them. You treat them with respect and dignity. You are the one that people come to see the most." I went home so happy and told Julian, "Guess what Dr. McDaniels said?" *That was pretty cool.* I don't like to sound like I'm bragging, and forgive me if I do sound that way, but it is true. I heard that I have some of the lowest numbers of clients who go into the hospital. Some sick people go in and out of the hospital as though it has revolving doors. For the most part, we manage to keep people out of the hospital. It's not just me, it's a team effort.)

Learning never ends, and I have learned from all of them. My work experience in this arena is extensive. For a decade now, I prescribe medications. I do psychiatric evaluations. I have responsibility for large numbers of inpatients as well as outpatients. I interview clients. I determine what their diagnoses are and give them medications to help them. And, yes, I treat everyone with respect, and a lot of that has to do with listening. I listen! I believe I'm imbued with great compassion. Much of it has come from my life experience, and I use it in the three roles I have been allotted: patient, healer, human being.

Psalms 91:2 says (KJV), "I will say of the Lord, He is my refuge and my fortress: my God; in him will I trust."

## Unrealistic Expectations

A moment ago, I wrote about putting people on pedestals and feeling betrayed by them. If you put your faith in people, thinking they belong on pedestals, you're probably going to be very disappointed too. Psalm 118:8 (*New Living Translation*) says, "It is better to take refuge in the Lord than to trust in people." When a person accepts Christ as Savior, that person is immediately indwelt by the Holy Spirit. From that moment on, nothing can separate us from God's love (see Romans 8:31-39). But what do you do after that? Spiritual maturity and growth depend on taking in Bible doctrine every day and applying it to your life. To make it "count," we need to open ourselves to God's truth daily by coming to him in a right manner. First John 1:9 says if we confess our sins, he is faithful and just to forgive us. This is a private matter between me and God that solely depends on God's grace. I may have to do this twenty times a day, but then I'm free to be filled with God's truth and be controlled by God the Holy Spirit instead of my old sin nature. It took a long time for me to learn this and practice the principle—but some people never do! They are "saved," but they still live in *the old self* being implacable, bitter, angry, resentful, and unforgiving. That person is "stuck," creating more problems for him or herself. Because of arrogance, people are unable to orient to God's grace—missing out on their personal potential in the plan of God. As R. B. Thieme Jr. would put it, that person is not living with a relaxed mental attitude and enjoying a personal love for God the Father that will sustain that person through any adversity.

Strangers or people you don't know very well should not disappoint. But sometimes they do too. My son died by suicide, and I was trying to tell somebody who asked me about Joe, sharing my feelings and grief, and she looked at her watch. You can't hold that against the individual. She is only a person, and so you just forgive her. But there are times when you want to scream. How could a person be so insensitive … so locked into herself and her needs? As soon as I realized I couldn't and shouldn't have false expectations or put loved ones on pedestals, I was no longer exposed to being dashed against the rocks until I bled. So many people who came to Joe's funeral sought us out to pay respects and were so very comforting. A few would say, "We'll call you." We realized we may not see or hear more from some of them even as they vowed otherwise.

## Seeing and Hearing

This is the way of things. But I am in *A Warm and Beautiful Place*. My relationship with the Lord sustains me. Of course, Julian and Jennifer were in horrific pain when Joe ended his life, and I do my best to share with them what I know. I do this gently. There's a song the Supremes sang, "You Can't Hurry Love." When a person loves someone they want to spend time with that person and learn all about them. It is the same way with God. You can't hurry this. It is a process. I may comment on the publication of a new book by Rick Hughes. In his book *Practicing Your Christianity*, for example, he entitled one chapter "Doing a Right Thing in a Right Way." That can spark interest. (How do you know when it's the right way?) Rick Hughes attributes R. B. Thieme Jr. with teaching him about many of the concepts he spotlights in this book. I like to hear what Julian thinks about these teachings. I ask. I listen. I turn on a K-Love radio station at home or in the car. It's a popular Christian broadcast station. I've been doing this for years, and so I hope and believe that Julian and Jennifer take some comfort in what they see and hear via these resources. A *New York Times* article I read centered on "The Science and Art of Listening" (http://nyti.ms/SAUCxo). Writer Seth S. Horowitz asks, "What do you hear right now?" Moments later, he comments, "By asking you what you were hearing, I prompted your brain to take control of the sensory experience—and made you listen rather than just hear." I pray the people I love do listen … not just hear.

# 3

## Mental Health:
## Let Your Strengths Define You

*We are never defeated unless we give up on God.*
—Ronald Reagan, president of the United
States of America, 1911-2004

People need to know that major mental illnesses are traceable to the same genetic variations. Among them are bipolar disorder, schizophrenia, depression, and ADHD (attention deficit hyperactivity disorder). Some people on both sides of our family have suffered with poor mental health. This did not bode well for our son, Joseph Julian Ackerley. Every day of Joe's adult life, he struggled bravely to fight off the demons associated with multiple psychiatric disorders and the side effects of some prescribed drugs.

Mental illness is the result of a sick brain, like diabetes is the result of a sick pancreas or cardiovascular disease a sick heart. In addition, a person may be responding only to external circumstances and be ignoring God. The Bible talks about depression and anxiety as a flawed relationship with God through human viewpoint. Mental instability results from relying on one's own strength and decision making instead of placing faith and hope in God. Joe tried so hard to stabilize himself; he was my hero. His death by suicide *eviscerated* me.

Joseph left a note. In part, it said, "Jesus is enough." Joseph loved The Lord with all his heart and soul. Jesus *is* enough, and in the end, God *wins*. Nothing can separate us from the Lord Jesus Christ. Joseph did not lose hope in God but he lost hope in his recovery.

We thank God for Joe's faith in Jesus Christ. In Romans 8:38-39, it says,

> And I am convinced that nothing can ever separate us from God's love. Neither death nor life, neither angels nor demons, neither our fears for today nor our worries about tomorrow—not even the powers of hell can separate us from God's love.

And that is a promise!

Msgr. Cahalane, at Our Mother of Sorrows Catholic Church, saw us the evening Joe died. He knew our grief was so deep he suggested we say the words, "Come, Lord Jesus, come," to help us get through moment by moment. Only God was holding me up so I could make it to the next minute.

At the time of Joe's death, I was a psychiatric nurse practitioner with a postmaster's certification. Yet I couldn't sufficiently help my own son, and that made me doubt my ability to help others. Ask my friends, and they will tell you that Julian and I did everything possible to help put Joe on a strong footing so he could be productive and enjoy life. We witnessed, firsthand, Joe's extreme mood swings, going from severe depression to mania, which is an expansive and grandiose mood, when he would sometimes go for days without sleep. Diagnoses included bipolar disorder, severe, with psychotic features: post-traumatic stress disorder, obsessive-compulsive disorder, panic disorder with agoraphobia, which means he had severe anxiety, making it difficult for him to be in crowds or close to people. And Joe had a substance-dependence disorder. From his teen years, looking back, I can see that he was attempting to "self-medicate" to alleviate some of his symptoms. Multiple medications were prescribed. Joe tolerated the side effects such as excessive weight gain, restlessness, and tremors. At times, he could barely hold a fork in his hand when it was time to eat.

(Thank you, Jesus)… We also witnessed progress toward well-being. We were proud of Joe for holding down a job for two consecutive years and for living in his own apartment. Joe delivered newspapers and a few times called his dad in the wee hours of winter days to come and meet him and help him finish his paper route. He was so overcome with anxiety and panic he could not finish the job. Julian didn't hesitate for a moment. Up and out he went. Of course, Joe could come *home* whenever he wanted to, and he had dinner with us many times each week. He wrote Christian rap music and poetry, and he loved the Lord. His death blindsided us. (Joe was taking lithium among other medications and stopped taking it on October 28, 2011. He died on January 20, 2012. He was off lithium for less than three months, and his life was over.) By this time, my faith in the Lord was very strong. Difficult as it may be for some people to understand, there's always a certain joy inside of me because I belong to the Lord, and he belongs to me. It's a sustaining force. It's like an anchor. I thank God for this. In a storm such as my son's suicide, the Lord sustained me.

It goes without saying I was not in this place with the Lord when I suffered a collapse years earlier when my children were very young.

The mental anguish I experienced then was excruciating, and after thirteen years of keeping things to myself, I reached briefly for illegal drugs to try and find some relief. I finally confided in a close friend, but she could not comprehend what I was going through. I had stayed silent and hid my despair for too long. This episode of trying to find relief was short-lived, a few months at the most, but long enough to wreak havoc with my body chemistry and toss me into what could have become an endless psychotic spiral downward. I mention this again to emphasize *that even when one's despair is a living hell, it's possible to climb out of that hell.* I believe this is the information the Lord wants me to share so that someone reading this book will be heartened—will know that even when a person hits bottom and continues to thud along on a downward trajectory, she can rebound. Even when your cherished child dies by suicide, you survive. My strong relationship with The Lord saved me and continues to guide me. It is a bond that defines me. But it isn't possible to wake up one morning and find your faith is ironclad. It takes time and practice, like working out in a gym takes time to build muscle and strength, so does a solid relationship with God. He will never abandon me, but I need to work on not abandoning him! I take in Bible doctrine every day.

## Lithium, Not New on the Scene

"We've known for half a century that lithium can control the mood extremes of bipolar disorder and lithium based drugs have been successfully used as therapy during that time" (see www.life-enhancement.com/magazine/article/952-can-lithium-benefit-brain-health).

Lithium has a suicide-preventing effect in the long-term treatment of affective (i.e. mood) disorders. According to many studies, it is the primary pharmacological answer to what can be done *now*. In a nutshell, as I write, it is still a treatment of choice and possesses properties that actually prevent suicide.

You may find this baffling if you are only familiar with lithium batteries! You may be surprised to discover that eggs, potatoes, and specific vegetables are some of the foods we eat that contain small amounts of lithium. Experts tell us we ingest only about two hundred to six hundred micrograms of lithium daily. Nine hundred milligrams per day may be the recommended dosage for a patient or client who must control the roller coaster rides associated with extreme mood swings. Some famous mineral springs in France (e.g., Vichy) were found to contain generous amounts of lithium. This may account for the feelings of extreme well-being about which those who bathed in these waters boasted. Records show that in the second century AD, the Greek physician Seranus Ephesios recommended "natural waters such as alkaline springs" as a treatment for mania. Remember these waters are believed to have contained higher amounts of lithium than other waters; and therein is (likely) the explanation for calming manic individuals and perking up depressed individuals. Spa clients drank the waters and soaked in them too.

I have seen the amazing results from lithium at work on the human brain! The dosage and length of time a person uses lithium must be carefully monitored, however, since lithium in high dosages can be toxic—deadly. And long before a client would be in mortal danger, he or she would probably experience unpleasant side effects such as dizziness, nausea, vomiting, thirst, tremors, and weight gain. Still no one should attempt to self-medicate with lithium.

I read an article about "Healing Waters" (www.csicop.org/sb/show/healing_waters_-_part__i_spas/), which contained an ominous note. According to Andrew Skolnick, "Levels of lithium that cause dangerous toxicity are rather close to therapeutic levels. This is especially so for people with severe cardiovascular or kidney disease. Therefore, it's likely that any natural waters with high enough lithium levels to have any beneficial psychological effect would also cause substantial illness and death."

If you read through the history of mineral springs and special waters in the United States of America, you come upon some baffling tales. It's almost as if someone is peddling "snake oil"—a "fix" for anything that ails you. Fact is, waters containing lithium did and do help many people feel good. That's an outcome that should not be tossed aside. I have used lithium to great advantage. After my manic episodes following the use of substances in 1986, I was hospitalized and started on lithium. After two months, I thought I was "cured," so I stopped taking the medication. I became manic again and had to be admitted to the hospital again. My mood stabilized, and so I was determined to stay on lithium and never stop taking it again. I never wanted to lose control and become manic again and have to be hospitalized. So I took lithium for the next *fifteen* years. Then I noticed I was feeling more jittery than usual. I would become quite nervous in settings that usually don't cause anxiety for me. My hair started falling out too! My thyroid was checked; lithium can affect the thyroid gland and the kidneys. The lab results of my TSH (i.e., thyroid stimulation hormone) were 15! The norm is 0.4-4. It was time to stop the lithium. There was not another medication that I felt comfortable about starting in its place so the psychiatrist said, "Let's wait and see." I waited for the other "shoe to fall," and that was over fifteen years ago. The mood swings never returned! To this day, I do not require medication for mood stabilization. I'm sure lithium had a part in that. Also God; God got me off the medication!

It's not widely understood why some patients stop taking lithium. Could it be unpleasant side effects? Could it be a person feels good and thinks the medicine is no longer necessary? Could it be there is a stigma attached to admitting reliance on lithium? For one of these reasons or all of these reasons or none of them, Joe stopped taking lithium, and we did not know it. Joe wanted to give plasma, which earned him thirty-five dollars per contribution. He had to be lithium-free, or they would not take his plasma. When I found out he had stopped taking it, I said, "Joe, your mood stabilization is more important than thirty-five dollars." That was probably the end of December 2011. He started taking it again, but it was too late. Three months later, this man who told us in no uncertain terms that he would never take his own life was dead.

"Perhaps the saddest irony of depression is that suicide happens when the patient gets a little better and can again function sufficiently" (Dick Cavett, entertainer). But God gives us dying grace too! You may already guess that Mr. Cavett has suffered from depression. He has discussed depression in print and on talk shows. Essentially, he first became aware of being clinically depressed when he was attending Yale. He is now in his seventies, and so he has lived with and managed it for a long time. He is a *stigma stomper* although he probably doesn't know anything about this label. By being candid about his (celebrity) depression, one might assume he helps to minimize the stigma for those who feel crushed by having to manage this burden.

## Move Along … Function

My faith in the Lord enabled me to go back to school when I was fifty-three years old and go back again when I was fifty-nine years old, and at the time, I was wondering if I could do this. I never thought I was smart enough to succeed. When I finally turned my life over to the Lord and said, "Okay, whatever you want me to do, I will do," I kept my word. From about age forty-nine to when Joseph died, I'd had that much experience to know that God's promises are true. I knew he'll always be there with me no matter what. I knew that if God calls you to do something, you can leave all the consequences to God. Dr. Charles Stanley says be obedient to God and leave all the consequences to him. Where the Lord guides, the Lord provides.

All the years of my youth, I had been committed to going to church without understanding that church alone is not enough. It took me spiraling down to "empty" to be ready to receive what I truly needed to be a whole and happy adult. I take no credit for finding the way; God's hand is in all of it.

## Mental Illness Can Be Fatal

People who suffer with mental illness often have other health problems. If, for example, a diabetic doesn't take care of himself, he is likely to suffer the damage that is predictable when the disease is out of control. A mentally ill person may die because he or she did not have the wherewithal to manage the diabetes, and so it ravished the body, and death resulted. A mentally ill person may hang out in sleazy environments, or get drunk and carelessly cross the street and get hit by a car. Maybe he or she was stabbed to death or overdosed. Studies tell us if you have a mental illness, your longevity is already cut off by fifteen to seventeen years due to the additional burden of illness and because of reckless situations you may get yourself into.

As we've seen, mental illness can lead to death by suicide. A person who is delusional, depressed, or in some out-of-control state is a few steps closer to that eventuality. Research shows that those who are severely depressed and who are using substances are at highest risk.

It's essential that we don't treat mental illness as something that belongs to the other guy—is another person's problem. Do we listen? Can we help? At the least, we can treat all people with respect. The Bible tells us we are all God's children. Respect may seem a small thing, but respect matters greatly. Even today when we believe more people are well-informed, in many quarters, there is shame and stigma attached to being mentally ill. Often mentally ill people neglect to bathe or shave, don't wear clean clothes—in short ... aren't well prepared to mingle in *polite company*. One client I'm especially fond of is a younger fellow who once gave me a hug. He reeked from cigarette smoke. But his hug was sweet to me. It was just after Joe passed away, and it reminded me of my son because he smokes the same brand of cigarettes that Joe smoked. That never-to-be-forgotten odor wafted up around me during that hug and made me smile. Others may not have welcomed the embrace!

Mentally ill people can't always be identified by behavior or physical appearance that "gives them away." And their challenges may be well controlled with therapy and drugs. Lithium, for example, has been valuable in stabilizing people who are bipolar and allowing those people to live a relatively normal life.

Something written by author Albert Camus really caught my attention: "Nobody realizes that some people expend tremendous energy merely to be normal." This has to be so for people who are hiding their afflictions from others. Each day these individuals monitor what they say and do so as to deflect suspicions that they are bipolar or depressed or worse. They fear they could lose a job or a promotion or be shunned if others knew the truth. Being on guard almost all the time has got to be exhausting.

In the book *Rebound and Keep Moving*, by R. B. Thieme Jr., he writes, "Sins are not only overt, but mental and verbal" (Prov. 6:17). When you meet a person and make a quick assessment, you could be mistaken. What you think about the person influences your behavior. If you don't want to send an inappropriate message, take care how you handle your thoughts. Or perhaps I should write … *take care how your thoughts handle you*. Mental attitude sins are just as bad as, if not worse than, others. (Rebound to get back in fellowship with God. Claim 1 John 1:9.) Recognize what you're thinking is wrong, give it to God, and move on. Open up the Holy Spirit so that God can fill you and work through you.

## Born Too Soon

*Studies reveal many who die by suicide were born prematurely—Joe was a* preemie. The studies tell us that the risk of mental disorders to those who were born prematurely is greater than to people who were born at full term. A normal full gestation term is from thirty-seven to forty-one weeks. Babies born at thirty-two to thirty-six weeks' gestation and have a genetic predisposition for mental illness were 1.6 times more likely than full-term babies to develop psychosis. You can read a synopsis of Chiara Nosarti's PhD study online. The Brain & Behavior Research Foundation is the source, and you'll find contact information in an appendix near the back of this book should you so desire (https://bbrfoundation.org/discoveries/premature-birth-heightens-risk-for-mental-illness).

"Brain scans of premature babies showed less connectivity between the brain's thalamus and specific regions of the cortex supporting higher mental functions." This information is attributable to researchers at King's College, London (www.techtimes.com/articles/50650/20150504/premature-birth-alters-brain-connection).

A touching poem written by Wendy Feireisen was sent to us after Joe died. This seems like a good time to share it with you:

*You don't get over it, you just get through it.*
*You don't get by it, because you can't get around it.*
*It doesn't "get better"; it just gets different.*
*Every day, Grief puts on a new face.*

## Two Years Later

An admirable and spiritual woman who has worked with Julian and whom we occasionally see socially phoned our house on July 16, 2014, to tell us that she had a dream and heard God very clearly. Her dream happened at three in the morning. God told her that Joseph was wrapped in his arms. He told her that Joseph benefitted someone else. I guess that would be me, because then I was a NP and talking about suicide with clients and their families, and Joe's death prepared me to more fully understand the depths of despair following a suicide. The Bible says, "Praise be to the God and Father of our Lord Jesus Christ, the Father of compassion and the God of all comfort, who comforts us in all our troubles, so that we can comfort those in any trouble with the comfort we ourselves received from God. For just as we share abundantly in the sufferings of Christ so also our comfort abounds through Christ" (2 Cor. 1:3-5, NIV). After she spoke with Julian, she spoke to me. It was two years after Joe died. She didn't know if we would be upset with her news. She repeated that she got this very strong message that God knew exactly what was going on. Joey is fine. She always called him Joey because she knew him since he was a little kid. He is in God's hands. And Jane can help many others through the experience. I told her this is wonderful news. I didn't doubt her for a minute. Hearing from God is not just a biblical times experience. God talks to people today through *his Word (e.g., Scripture)*. I know that first-hand. I was really appreciative of what she was telling me. It was a great comfort.

## Smart Guy!

Joe was very intelligent! He had a high IQ. He earned three associate degrees and one certification from Pima Community College in Tucson. He framed the diplomas and certificate and hung them on the wall of his room at our house. I know he was proud of his accomplishments, and so were we:

1) Associate of General Studies
2) Associate of Liberal Arts
3) Associate of Science
4) AGEC-S Certification

## Can Love Be Cruel? You Betcha!

When a person is "different," he easily draws unwanted attention to himself. Perhaps he speaks too loudly or has a strange "look" about him, which is often a side effect of medication he must take to keep the demons at bay. I think we can all agree this is not surprising, but sometimes even close relatives can be thoughtless even though they are aware of the sick person's struggles … what then? Joe was the victim of cruel comments and thoughtless acts, and he knew full well; he was not invited to attend some family functions. In short, he was shunned by some. Imagine how that added to his burden? My heart cried for him. Misunderstanding mental illness and lack of knowledge about psychiatric disorders will only contribute to marginalizing the people who need our acceptance and help. On the other hand, there were family members; a few friends; individual doctors; nurse practitioners; case managers; and behavioral health workers who were sincere and empathetic and who cared for, protected, and tried to help Joseph. This wasn't easy. A fine line exists between enabling (doing something for Joe that he should and could do for himself) and helping (doing something for him that he was not capable of doing himself). Nothing about coping with mental illness is easy!

## Stigma Stompers

Stigma as defined by the dictionary is "a mark of disgrace of infamy; a stain or reproach, as on one's reputation" (http://dictionary.reference.com/browse/stigma).

You can see why we would want to stomp on it—finish it off, banish it. On a very practical level, the stigma or perceived stigma may serve to prevent someone who suffers from seeking help. That can be the unkindest cut of all.

Joe and I were official Stigma Stompers! This grew out of our involvement with NAMI, National Alliance on Mental Illness.

"It is a grassroots mental health organization dedicated to building better lives for the millions of Americans affected by mental illness" (https://www.nami.org/About-NAMI). NAMI works to raise public awareness, and Joe and I participated in NAMI Walks in Tucson. These walks are organized annually, and members of our family were always there with Joe. It's a big deal, and thousands of people attend. I have a photograph of former congresswoman Gabbie Giffords with Joe. Giffords was a speaker at a NAMI gathering. You may recall, on January 8, 2011, at a "Congress on Your Corner" event in Tucson, Giffords was shot in the head. Remarkably, she survived the assassination attempt, and although she relinquished her position in Washington, she said, "I will return, and we will work together for Arizona and this great country."

The shooter was identified as schizophrenic and mentally unfit for trial. If you look back at the media coverage, you'll find the shooter repeatedly showed signs of mental illness in the many months that preceded this treacherous act. Six people were murdered and many injured.

One cannot help but wonder why this shooter wasn't stopped long before he committed murder and mayhem. Were all those people who were witness to his sickness reluctant to speak out, reluctant to stop him from advancing further into his madness, owing to the stigma attached to mental breakdown? Could this horror have been avoided if the general public was better informed and mental illness—especially severe mental illness was not so laden with *fear* so that no one spoke? Surely, warning and prevention opportunities were ripe for action many times over, but they were never utilized. How would history have been written if the heinous crime never occurred?

On December 10, 2012, I wrote to Gabby, "My husband and I attended the movie *Lincoln* two weeks ago, and we were very surprised when you and your family took the seats right in front of us. I have admired your courage in the recovery process following the tragic event of January 2011, and was happy to see you enjoying the movie with your family." I wrote more about the 2009 Stigma Stompers gathering and NAMI (National Alliance on Mental Illness), and I took the opportunity to add, "You may know that individuals with mental illness have a higher rate of death than the general population, and suicide is one way that people with mental illness lose decades of potential life." I went on to suggest that Gabby may want to use her influence to change attitudes and cultural beliefs regarding mental illness.

## Faith Based Principles and Mental Illness

Dr. David Sherwood, professor at Baylor University, wrote, "Deliberately avoiding spiritual and religious issues is professional incompetence" (see Ethical Integration of Faith and Social Work Practice: Evangelism Spring 2002, 29:1). He is one expert who espouses the role *faith* plays in a clinical practice. Of course, one must consider the subject of interweaving faith in Christian and Non-Christian settings. (See p. 7 "Integrating Faith-Based Principles with Clinical Mental Health Issues, A Christian Approach for Improving Treatment Outcomes by Craig A. Miller, MS, LMSW, ACSW).

The above mentioned report discusses what hinders us from integrating faith with mental health practice. After all, therapy is based on dealing with personal issues. Why fear imposing personal faith unless the fear originates out of a personal struggle with the integrating faith? The practitioner must be mindful of motives. The comfort a client experiences from his or her relationship with God can be especially meaningful in times of trouble.

You know how I feel about the Lord and my relationship with him, so when a client tells me he or she is a Christian, an opportunity may present itself to pray together right there in my office.

Experts tell us that "praying affects epinephrine and other steroid messengers or stress hormones, leading to lower blood pressure, more relaxed heart rate and respiration, and other benefits."

One study concludes, "Eighty-two percent of Americans believe in the healing power of prayer. Sixty-three percent of patients want their doctors to discuss matters of faith. Ninety-nine percent of physicians say religious beliefs make a positive contribution to healing." These observations are attributable to Duke University research. You can read similar opinions at http://prayersandapples. com/faith-and-healing-time-magazine/.

## CARF Regulations

CARF (Commission on the Accreditation of Rehabilitation Facilities) is an international regulation agency. One must demonstrate high standard of care to addicts, alcoholics, and others seeking help in order to be endorsed by CARF. One of the important CARF regulations explains how to proceed if a client wants to pray or doesn't want to pray. It is understood that a person's faith could play an important role in discussions between a person and his or her provider.

I did a psychiatric evaluation yesterday. The client is having a horrible time and is depressed. She hasn't been on her medication for three weeks, and one of my questions was, do you have any sense of spirituality? She said, "I used to be a Catholic, but I don't believe in God anymore." The client did not want to pursue that avenue, and so we moved on. Someone else might say to me, I'm a Christian.

And then I ask, "Do you have a church you go to?" That can be really helpful in this time of need, and then we open up and talk about that.

And in my office at work I've got a bulletin board, and nobody ever said anything negative about the spiritual "God messages" I have posted. Some clients look at the messages, which are primarily Bible quotations. I've been in that office for seven years. I have a lot of people asking to see me. This isn't really about me … It's about the Holy Spirit working through me. I listen to people. I love people. It's an impersonal love. It comes through God. I might not like that person, but the Holy Spirit loves *the person to pieces*. One of my clients just said to me, "I love you, Jane," and I said, "I love you too, Maria." People want to give me hugs all the time. I'm willing to be *broken bread and poured-out wine* for others. God is using me; he is using me up. But it is so neat because he keeps filling me up. I talk to about ten to fifteen people a day who are struggling with a serious mental illness. I love it. It's the most wonderful job, and everyone has a different problem, and I listen to each person and work with each person, and we negotiate on the medications we're going to prescribe. There is a placebo effect with medications too. If you like me and I give you a medication, that medication is going to work better for you than if someone else (you didn't believe had genuine feelings for your best interests) gave it to you. There are some studies that bring this information to the forefront.

One of the doctors I admire most tells us, "You have got to love your patients. You've got to give them hope. Give them encouragement. They don't have anything." He's speaking, especially, of the indigent individuals. They don't have money. They have to decide whether to buy their medication or pay their electric bill. They are just down-and-out, and they live in terrible places. There are gunshots going off all the time. People are getting raped. Little kids go and play hide-and-seek, and the adult man who finds them molests them. Just horrible stories and you're listening to all those bits and pieces, and now here they're sitting in your office depressed, and they have PTSD (i.e., post-traumatic stress disorder), and they can't sleep at night, and I'm listening to all these unhappy facts. If they hold a job for six months or a year, we give them a pat on the back. And you know it is so worthy of praise. They got a job at Wendy's or a job at the carwash detailing cars. *Congratulations are in order!*

From my own experience, I know some professionals tune out and tune in to themselves. They're thinking about how long until they can break for lunch, or they're thinking about their stock investment portfolio. In short, they are not focused on helping the person who has a severe mental illness. I remember one psychiatric provider whom I went to see years ago. He interrupted me while I was in crisis in his office because he had to take a phone call. Apparently, he was involved in a land purchase, and that was his priority. He made it abundantly clear that I could wait. His behavior did not befit a skilled and capable doctor, and I hope there aren't many like him, but such practitioners do exist.

I have some words from Deuteronomy 31:6 printed and placed on my desk where I can see them. I sometimes share the verse with my clients. "Be strong and courageous. Do not be afraid or terrified because of them, for the LORD your God goes with you; he will never leave you nor forsake you."

*A client is a person and not a disease!*

I heard a physician in a hospital ask about the appendix in 417. The person who answered knew exactly what the doctor meant. There was, however, a *person* in 417 who happened to have an appendix or perhaps did not have one any longer. This two-party conversation demonstrated the insensitivity or, perhaps more accurately, the ignorance of the speakers.

When you're working with people who have mental illness, they are probably treated like a "thing" and not a person by many people they encounter. I know this full well because it happened to me. I fully embrace the person-centered therapy approach to all my clients when possible. It is not possible when someone is so sick he or she is hallucinating or screaming or in some other way, completely out of control. Still, even then, we are dealing with a person!

## Person-Centered vs. Illness-Centered Therapy

I focus on a relationship with a patient. The diagnosis is not or should not be a stand-alone (*I am not referring to the person as "the appendix in 417"*)!

This means beginning our meeting with welcoming the individual and engaging them in conversation. A message in the lunch room at La Frontera Southwest clinic spells out what person-centered care is all about. It goes something like this:

> Illness-centered meeting: begins with illness assessment
> *Person-centered*: services are based on personal suffering and help needed
> Illness-centered: diagnosis and treatment needed
> *Person-centered*: work toward quality of life goals
> Illness-centered: work toward illness-reduction goals
> *Person-centered*: treatment and rehabilitation are goal driven
> Illness-centered: symptom driven and rehabilitation is disability driven
> And so it goes.

## Give a Man a Fish

Maimonides, a revered philosopher, put the spotlight on this way of thought when he told us: "Give a man a fish and you feed him for a day. Teach a man to fish and you feed him for a lifetime."

Mark Ragins, MD, writes at length about this approach (mragins@mhala.org). He stresses never giving up on someone and never letting them give up on themselves. I like that! He puts the spotlight on recovery. His book *A Road to Recovery* is available at www.village-isa.org.

Dr. Ragin has written many papers for those of us who work with people who have severe mental illnesses. On more than one occasion, a medical director I worked with distributed copies of a particular report to all psychiatric providers. On one copy, he wrote, "Please read this whole thing. It might make you a better provider of care." His emphasis that day was to think about and deliver a more person-centered approach to caring for our clients. (You may have noticed I use the terms *clients* and *patients* interchangeably. In some clinics, management directs staff to say *patients*, and in other clinics, management favors the use of the word *clients*.)

I find Dr. Ragin's observations and comments to be refreshing. "After a while, I realized that people weren't always taking medications in the careful way I was prescribing them." He went on to explain possible reasons this could be, and he included what he thought he could do to help. He reasoned a person might not know how to find a drugstore, and he handed out maps that showed the location of pharmacies. He handed out pillboxes to help a person keep track of pills and arranged to have someone work with a person's insurance company to make sure bills were paid.

## Stop and Think

I know firsthand how a patient feels. We must treat clients with respect and compassion. A man felt he could never be forgiven because he had killed a person. A woman had an abortion and was in despair, feeling overwhelming guilt and that she was beyond God's forgiveness. "Will you pray with me, Jane?" Sometimes I am asked by my clients to do that. We close our eyes and pray together. I lift them up to the Lord with their heavy burdens that the Lord can lighten. Jesus took care of all our sins on the cross, past, present, and future. He accepts us just as we are. It may help to talk about that.

# 4

## Education: Keep It Coming

*The mind is not a vessel to be filled, but a fire to be kindled.*
—Plutarch

God told me to become a doctor. *What?*

At 3:00 a.m., I received the Lord's instruction: *look into getting a doctorate.* It was so impractical. I have a husband. I have children. I have a job. It's expensive. I'm not smart enough. There will be a ton of reading and tests where I will be timed. I'm too old for this.

Nevertheless, I attended Texas Christian University online.

I worked and attended school, and then there was only time for study. I couldn't even go to a movie with my husband. But I knew … where the Lord guides, the Lord provides … and the rest, as they say, is history. *Sometimes when I reflect on the past, I realize God rescued me by sending me off to get more education. This was my medicine when Joseph died. I kept working on earning my doctorate.*

I've had numerous 3:00 a.m. visits from the Lord in which he speaks to my soul. Once when Julian and I traveled to Israel with a group of Christian people, another traveler revealed that she knew all about the 3:00 a.m. visits. She too gets spoken to regularly at that surprising hour.

In my younger years, it wasn't unusual for me to start my day at 5:00 a.m. And I knew I was going to spend most of it studying.

I had to end my piano lessons as I worked for the doctorate, but you already know I returned to them once my studies were completed.

## God Spottings

When our children were little, I read the book *Children: The Challenge*, by child psychiatrist Rudolf Dreikurs, MD with Vicki Soltz, RN. The subtitle is *Work on Improving Parent-Child Relations— Intelligent, Humane and Eminently Practical*. It helped me as a mom, but it also was instrumental in leading to my life's work, which, of course, has everything to do with mental health and psychiatry. I recognized the Lord's hand in this. He scatters crumbs in our paths.

I keep a journal entitled "God Spottings." It is a great way for me to be reminded about all the things our Lord does for us or for others about whom we care. For example, I have a prayer list on the refrigerator door, which is in our kitchen. I call it my 24/7 prayer list. When I tell someone, "I'll pray for you," I mean it. I put the person's name on the list so I don't forget, and I pray for the individual. Usually, it's a prayer for someone to get well. When the list grows long, as it often does, I simply pray for our Lord to answer the prayers of everyone on my prayer list. From time to time, I look over the list and realize prayers have been answered. That is a God Spotting!

## Julian's Fifty-first Birthday

Julian really wanted tickets to see the play *Wicked* while we were in New York. There were none to be had except the three-hundred-dollar variety, but Jennifer knew of a lottery that took place just before the show. Julian and Jen put their names into it, and out of hundreds of names, Jen's name was drawn! We got two twenty-five-dollar tickets in the front row to see *Wicked* on Julian's birthday! Jen had seen it already the previous March, and so she stood in the TKTS line to get us tickets for *Fiddler* (with Harvey Fierstein), and Julian and I saw the show. It was fabulous. Thank you, Jennifer. Thank you, God!

Here are more examples. One, my grandmother's grave is in South Lawn Cemetery. Julian and I were at the cemetery to visit my father's grave, and I thought of my grandmother who died a long time ago. Since the grave markers are on stones that are flush with the ground and it's not easy to read them, I said, "Lord, could you just lead me to Grandma Shinevar's grave?" I had no clue where it was, and the Lord caused me to turn around and walk a few steps in that new direction, and suddenly, there was my grandma's grave. Now that's a God Spotting! He is there for me for the big times and the small things too. Another time I got lost. Julian and I were at a football game. The place was crowded, and I had gone to the ladies' restroom. When I came out, I didn't see Julian. After a while, I asked, "Lord, would you help me to find Julian? We need to be leaving together." I hung around for a minute or two, and all of a sudden, here comes Julian. I was so happy and knew I had another God Spotting for my journal. I could go on and on, but let me just mention one more God Spotting. I needed to make a presentation at a gathering in Louisiana, and Julian was going with me. When I got onto the plane, I thought Julian was right behind me! But he was in the men's room, and he missed the plane. I ended up in Louisiana all by myself. I had to get a car and wait for Julian because I thought he would be on the very next plane arriving (he wasn't), and then we had to drive to New Orleans. For some reason, I had made arrangements for us to fly to Baton Rouge instead of New Orleans. Those cities are about eighty miles apart. I got there about 2:00 p.m., and Julian didn't get in until about 8:00 p.m. I drove around, found a place to eat and places to explore, looked around, and listened to Christian music. When Julian's plane landed, I picked him up in the rental car. Most of this *activity* represented new and unfamiliar experiences for me. In the Bible, Paul talks about being comfortable in any situation. I see God's hand in my "adventure"—clearly another God Spotting.

It showed me I was able to carry on. "I can do all things through Christ which strengthens me" (Phil. 4:13, KJV).

This is a good time to mention Julian was always supportive of me. That's not true about everyone I knew. When I asked God about all the negativity I was hearing from others *(Nonsense, you're too old to go back to school. You're just wasting money. Who would hire you after you earn your degree? Younger people would step to the head of the line, and there you would be, just feeling poorly about the whole thing)*, do you know what the Lord told me? "Don't listen!"

Here are some notes I made in a personal notebook ten years ago:

- God is completely sovereign (controls all).
- He is infinitely wise (knows all).
- He loves us perfectly (always does the right thing for us).

I know these things to be true today. You already know *I did not listen* to the naysayers.

## Straight As

You may want to classify this as a God Spotting too. Maybe yes. Maybe no. When I earned my doctorate degree, we attended the graduation ceremonies. I was dressed in traditional cap and gown. I had received As and, therefore, was graduating with honors. This entitled me to wear a special cord with my graduation gown. I did not have one like the other people who were receiving their advanced degrees. It seems the school authorities inadvertently did not send the memorandum to me that was sent to all doctoral seniors, and I did not order the cord. "Humble yourselves therefore under the mighty hand of God, that he may exalt you in due time." You'll find these words in 1 Peter 5:6.

Coach John Wooden (1910-2010) offered a "Be humble" comment that I also remember: "Talent is God given. Be humble. Fame is man given. Be grateful. Conceit is self-given. Be careful."

The other day, I was looking at my prayer journal (Jennifer gave it to me as a gift for my fifty-first birthday). I noticed some comments I included about humility.

> Jesus humbled himself, and we must do the same. He said, "Follow me," and we must try to be like him. God has goals for each of us and those that apply to all of us. Walk in a matter worthy of Jesus Christ. Put on kindness … humility, forgiveness. Put on love. Don't do anything out of emptiness of prideful conceit but rather of humility of mind. (We're not #1.) We should think of others first. Put aside all wickedness in humility and receive the word of God; (to understand God's word) clothe yourself in humility. Dress yourself in the spirit of humility/ Christian grace, Christian humility. Others will see the humility. If I see it, it's probably not there.

I filled several pages of my prayer journal with observations about humility. I made them stand out by marking the margins with black ink: *Humility/Spirit of Humility*. I'm many years beyond that birthday and have filled all the pages of that journal, and it is useful to be reminded about the importance of humility.

Here's another way to think about it …

> *There is nothing noble in being superior to your fellow man;*
> *true nobility is being superior to your former self.*
> —Ernest Hemingway

# 5

## My Utmost for His Highest

These words make up the title of a book that is considered to be one of the most popular Christian books ever written. The title comes from many sermons Oswald Chambers delivered. The book's publication date is 1924. The 415-page book reportedly has been translated into more than thirty-nine languages. It contains 365 sections—one for each day of the year and is meant to be read daily for inspiration.

Not too long ago, God wanted me to be a speaker. I said, "Okay, God, if you want me to be a speaker, you've got to find me someplace to speak, 'cause no one is asking me." About two weeks later, a good friend called me and asked if I would speak to an occupational nursing group. I said, "Sure." I talked about mental illness and psychotic disorders and medications. I talked about how the proper medications could keep a person who is diagnosed as bipolar out of the hospital. I discussed the roles lithium plays in suicide treatment and prevention. This audience deserved to hear something that would enrich them. I did not want to waste their time.

I would like to talk about this book *A Place That's Warm and Beautiful.* I would travel to speak to audiences everywhere. I would give my utmost for his highest. The book is intended to help people. I reveal deep, dark wounds. Readers "see me" out of control and discover that when I was limping along on empty, I turned to God.

There was no one else. My relationship with the Lord finally began in earnest, and everything got better. Will my story inspire others? God told me to go to school, be a speaker, get my doctorate, and write a book. I did. *Nothing that happens is accidental.*

The Lord is awesome!

## Who Is in Charge?

I'm an in-charge kind of person, but when I decided to write my doctoral thesis on *prayer*, I soon learned God wanted me to write it on *suicide*. You know who won out.

Industrialist Henry Ford said, *"I believe God is managing affairs and that He doesn't need any advice from me. With God in charge, I believe everything will work out for the best in the end. So what is there to worry about?"*

This instruction to write about suicide came about before we lost our son, Joseph. I had absolutely no hint that we would soon be up close and personal with the death by suicide of our son. I spent one year researching and writing a paper that fills forty pages. A short version, totaling seven pages, will ultimately be available for reading on the web. As of this writing, it will be posted on *advance* for NPs and PAs' website. If you're eventually surfing the Internet for information about suicide, you may locate it.

Here are seven of the points you'll find on those seven pages:

1) Psychiatric disorders are present in 90 percent of suicides.
2) Psychiatric disorders, including depression, are chronic and recurrent. Access to treatment is essential in decreasing rates of suicide.
3) There is a need to link people at risk to support systems that foster confidentiality, privacy, and trust.
4) Prevention or reduction in the number of suicides was demonstrated when access to a specific suicide method was restricted, when telephone contact or other means of con-

tact was utilized, and when educational intervention targeted primary care providers.

5) Many researchers agreed that telephone intervention and follow-up contact (by well-trained and highly capable respondents) could reduce rates of suicide, reduce hospital readmission, and increase medication compliance.

6) Psychiatric disorders are underrecognized and undertreated in primary care.

7) Suicide remains a sensitive issue in all countries.

# CDC

The Centers for Disease Control and Prevention tracks figures of Americans who die by suicide, and the numbers are likely to surprise. In 2013, for example, over forty-one thousand suicides were reported. This same source tells us suicide is the tenth leading cause of death for Americans.

Clearly, it is an important public health problem, but did you know it? People may be reluctant to talk about it since victims are subject to blame and those closest to them; family and friends are stigmatized. *Why didn't you know? Why didn't you do something? How could you let that happen?*

The National Council for Suicide Prevention website (www.thencsp.org) offers five ways we can work to eliminate stigma along with additional information.

1) *Learn the facts.* You won't pass along information that isn't accurate and can be damaging.

2) *Talk about it.* People will know they aren't alone and that there are people who are well trained and sympathetic to the needs of everyone involved (i.e., the person who contemplates death by suicide, family, friends, and coworkers).

3) *Support someone who is struggling.* A knee-jerk reaction is to run away. *This is crazy. I'm outta here.* Resist that urge

and let the individual know "fault" is not and should not be the issue. Just like a person with diabetes needs help to manage the challenge, so too does a person need help if he or she entertains thoughts of suicide. Help is available, and it is possible for the troubled individual to get back to a good place—the life he/she wants to live. Your encouragement lets in a little ray of hope where there was none.

President John Fitzgerald Kennedy said, *"Every area of trouble gives out a ray of hope; and the one unchangeable certainty is that nothing is certain or unchangeable."* I would have told Mr. Kennedy that the death by suicide of a loved one is certain and is unchangeable … but it is possible to keep another person from going down that road. This knowledge is my *ray of hope*.

4) *Correct negative stereotypes when you see them in the media.* Imagine how letters to the editor, for example, can help put the focus on restoring mental well-being and reach out to people who suffer and feel hopeless and who fear they are alone. Movies and television scripts that wrongly dramatize mental illness can frighten viewers. If sufferers are portrayed as dangerous misfits or worse, then compassionate care and concern may be withheld. Be quick to praise the *flip side* of the issue. The media can be a great ally in combating the stigma that shrouds mental illness. Letters that say, "Thank you," for shining a light on positive outcomes should help to promote more of the same.

5) *Challenge negative stereotypes wherever you find them*—at home, at work, in the classroom.

"Let each of you look not only to his own interests, but also to the interests of others" (Phil. 2:4).

## Prevention Resources

September 10 is World Suicide Prevention Day. The purpose of this day and designation is to raise awareness around the globe that suicide can be prevented.

*"Perhaps the saddest irony of depression is that suicide happens when the patient gets a little better and can again function sufficiently,"* wrote talk show host, author, and entertainer Dick Cavett. Cavett is currently in his late seventies, but he did stand-up comedy for a time, and I was surprised to read he had his own bouts with depression. (I almost wrote "severe" depression, but I caught myself. All depression is severe. Some more, some less, but depression should not be ignored.) So did and do many other well-known people have to deal with depression, and when they step forward and talk about their battles, it can be a source of encouragement to listeners who know all too well what they mean. I have listed some well-known people who died by suicide a little further along in this book. Cavett's statement should make people sit up and take notice. Those of us who love and treat depressed people must never allow ourselves to be lulled into a mind-set of complacency. Famous people who seem to have everything one could want can be depressed! They too may struggle with demons! They too fight the good fight and many succumb anyway. This tragedy (death by suicide) plays no favorites. So make no mistake about it … you are not alone, and if you find that a comforting thought … *lean on it*, and don't hesitate to reach out for help.

> *I think that is what we all want to hear; that we are not*
> *alone in hitting the bottom and that it is possible to come*
> *out of that place courageous, beautiful and strong.*
> —Anna White, author

# 6

## Forgiveness: A Simple Concept

*Forgiveness is an act of the will, and the will can function regardless of the temperature of the heart.*
—Corrie Ten Boom, author

There is no room for hate in your heart, in your life. I know this! It is repeated over and over in the Bible, and yet how could I forgive family members for ostracizing Joe and making him feel so badly? People he loved caused him such grief. When I think about it logically, I must conclude they didn't know better. Perhaps they were afraid for him—for us all. But I don't have to search for understanding. I just have to forgive, because the Lord would not have it any other way.

An article in a Mayo Clinic newsletter written by staff states, "Forgiveness doesn't mean that you deny the other person's responsibility for hurting you, and it doesn't minimize or justify the wrong. You can forgive the person without excusing the act. Forgiveness brings a kind of peace that helps you go on with life" (www.mayoclinic.org/health-lifestyle/adult-health/in-depth/forgiveness/art-20047692). Corrie Ten Boom said it so well (I quote her at the start of this chapter), *"Forgiveness is an act of the will, and the will can function regardless of the temperature of the heart."*

Corrie Ten Boom was a brave Christian woman who helped save Jews from Hitler's death camps. She is an author and has written that, in her postwar experience, those who were able to forgive Nazi brutality were best able to rebuild their lives.

Corrie and her sister, Betsie, had been arrested and put into Ravensbruck, a concentration camp, because they concealed Jews in their home during the Nazi occupation of Holland. Her sister died there. And prior to death, she starved and suffered other atrocities. Corrie wrote about this in an article in the magazine *Guideposts*. She told of speaking to one group of people in Germany about forgiveness. "The solemn faces stared back at me, not quite daring to believe. There were never questions after a talk in Germany in 1947. People stood up in silence, in silence collected their wraps, in silence left the room." Corrie recognized a man in the audience who had been a guard where her sister and she had been incarcerated. She remembered him and the leather crop swinging from his belt. He approached her and asked if she would forgive him. At first, she could not. "Betsie had died in that place. Could he erase her slow terrible death simply for the asking?" Finally, the author knew she had to forgive. She writes that not only is this a message from God, but she had a home in Holland for victims of Nazi brutality and had seen firsthand how those who could forgive, who did forgive, were able to return to the outside world and function. They were the only ones who moved on.

## Benefits

I forgive because Jesus forgave us. End of discussion. But I noticed that when I forgave, I no longer felt like a victim. The people who hurt Joe and who hurt me lost power over me as soon as I forgave them. Is my health more robust now than before? It is. I have noticed this as I write this book. Writing gives me the luxury of concentrating on things that would otherwise be stored in the recesses of the past. Perhaps that is another reason God told me to write a book. The Lord wants me to pay attention to how good it feels to not hold a grudge. I do my best to point this out to clients: let go of anger; make room for forgiveness to take root.

In my job as a psychiatric nurse practitioner, I see people every day and understand when they tell me this medication causes memory loss; this medication causes me to feel like a zombie. The medication makes my mouth really dry. These things happened to me when I was taking medications. But I also know—without a doubt—that a personal relationship with the Lord is something that can restore you … pump new life into you … set you up to live a productive and happy life. I know this because it happened to me.

*Matthew West Lyrics*

> Show me how to love the unlovable
> Show me how to reach the unreachable
> Help me now to do the impossible

You can listen to Matthew West sing his song "Forgiveness" via YouTube. He also tells the story of how he came to write this song. Forgive me please if I remain a little mysterious here; I won't try to relate this information to you. I invite you to find it for yourself. The person who inspired Mr. West was someone who suffered a tragic loss, and one would wonder how she could bring herself to forgive the perpetrator. She did. Fact is, I come upon stories like this more often than you may guess.

⁓⁊⁊⁓

God forgets about our sins. See the *King James Bible*, "I, even I, am he that blotteth out thy transgressions for mine own sake, and will not remember thy sins." If we confess our sins, he is faithful and just to forgive us our sins and to cleanse us from all unrighteousness—those sins we remember and those that we don't remember.

## Patience

One of my favorite prayers is the *Serenity Prayer*. You probably know it: "God grant me the serenity to accept the things I cannot change; Courage to change the things I can; and wisdom to know the difference."

The original words are attributed to the Christian writer and theologian Reinhold Neibuhr (1892-1971). There are more words in this prayer, but some believe they were added at a later date (see www.living-prayers.com/topics/serentiy_prayer.html). As I was preparing to write this memoir, I noticed that I filled pages in my prayer journal with comments on patience. For example, patience is not a gift. It's a fruit of the spirit, and it's important … Wait for God to supply. Wait for God's timing. Wait for what God wants to give. Develop calmness and a quiet way to proceed. The willingness to wait for God's plan and purpose is essential for obedience to God. Wait and listen to God. When we choose to step ahead of God's timing, there are consequences. Samuel and Saul tried to kill David. They consulted with a medium (i.e., fortune-teller) to find out what is going to happen, and both Saul and son ended up dying. When we face difficulties in life, we have the opportunity to learn how to be patient.

Helen Keller said, "We could never learn to be brave and patient if there were only joy in the world."

As I write, I realize, my personal patience quotient has risen, but mastery is not yet completely within my grasp.

## Meditation

When I look at my prayer diary entry dated 2/8/2005, I notice I wrote, "Our personal time with Jesus, being close to him, reading scripture and being absorbed with him. Be consistent about it. Meditate day and night." I made these notes more than ten years ago, but I should not refer to them now without telling you I attribute this *enlightenment* to Charles Stanley. I even jotted the benefits that would ensue:

1) You will learn to develop a quiet spirit. On the inside, you are quiet.
2) A purifying of heart will take place if things we are doing don't fit us. They will be eliminated.
3) A deepening of hunger for God (when you fall in love with someone, you want to spend more time with that someone).
4) It will enlarge your view of God and help you to know that from God's point of view, things are small.
5) Verses become familiar (memorized).
6) Clarifies direction for our lives. (What does God want us to do?)
7) Confirm counsel. Affirm others counsel by God.
8) Confidence is obtained. We team up with omnipotent God. My confidence is in God.

I went on with further entries about meditation and then wrote, "Challenge, sit five minutes with your eyes closed. Quiet and seclusion. I underscored the words: *seclusion*, *silence* (in my head!), and *self-control.*

*Half an hour's meditation each day is essential, except when you are busy. Then a full hour is needed.* These words are attributed to Saint Francis de Sales.

Is this impractical advice? What do you think?

I shared these observations with my prayer diary over ten years ago, and it's as though I wrote them yesterday. I've learned more since then, but nothing I have learned makes me want to alter any of these statements. If anything has changed, it is that I'm more indebted than ever to following the path that opened up my personal relationship with the Lord. Most of these rituals are as natural to me as inhaling and exhaling. I just do it!

I found a note at the very end of this journal dated January 4, 2001. It is as follows:

*My Dearest Jennifer,*

*I'm having great difficulty putting all my feelings into words. You have been a joy and inspiration in my life since the day you were born.*

*Looking through the pictures now, I'm reminded of many of the things you stand for: friendship, adventure, family, talent, growth and maturity, beauty, love, boyfriends and many different hair-dos! You mean all those things to me and more.*

*Jennifer, you've matured into a beautiful, talented, spirit filled young woman. You have so much from which to choose because you've kept an open mind and healthy spirit. It is obvious that the love of God has touched you and continues to guide you through your life. You've had an ongoing relationship with Him that is so special and personal. It is obvious that God loves you by the way He shines through your eyes.*

*I love you, too, Jennifer. I feel so blessed to have a wonderful daughter like you. You have made my life special, too, just by being here.*

*All my love,*
*Mom*

---

Famous People Who Died by Suicide
  Vincent Van Gogh
  Vivian Leigh
  Carrie Fisher
  Robin Williams
  Linda Hamilton
  Virginia Woolf
  Ernest Hemingway

# 7

## Joe and I Were Buddies

*Written May 11, 2008*

> *Dear Mom,*
>
> *Thank you for being such a blessing in my life, and such a great friend. Keep sharing your Faith to all who listen. You touch lives with the Holy Spirit! I love you, Joseph.*

*Joe wrote these words in a card he gave to me. He wrote touching notes in the cards he sent to Julian and Jennifer too.*

It's only fitting that at least one chapter in *A Place That's Warm and Beautiful* be devoted to discussing the happiness surrounding times spent with our dear son (and brother) Joseph Julian Ackerley. He was a fun-loving guy. He and I would go to the park where he could zoom up and down a cement ramp on his skateboard. Joe and I rode bicycles together, played guitars together, and rode around together in his goofy cars. I always told him he should write a book about all his car adventures. At one time or another, Joe had Volkswagens, the Celica, the Civic, the Toyota Tacoma, the Maxima, and the big Town Car, in which he liked to *chauffeur* Julian and me around town. I especially like to remember the story about the car that wouldn't go in reverse. Joe and I parked on University Avenue one day, heading straight into the parking space, and when we left, we had to open the front doors of the car and, on each side, stick out our feet and push on the ground to get the car to go backward. Of course, university students were sitting at a sidewalk café watching us. Everyone had a good laugh.

I don't have a keen sense of direction when I'm out driving. Joseph frequently led the way and helped me with directions. He was a gentle and sensitive person, and when I practiced playing the piano and he was trying to rest, I would ask him if my playing the piano would bother him. "Music to my ears, Mom," he would say with a smile even though I knew he frequently wasn't feeling well and was stretched out on the sofa to rest.

Julian was thrilled to have Joe in the Boys Chorus. His presence made four of the tours especially exciting. Joe participated in the tour to Washington, DC, to sing in the White House for President Bush Sr., and he went with the Chorus to Australia, New Zealand, and Hawaii. When Joseph had outgrown the choristers, he maintained a connection by being involved in the Alumni Chorus. He attended concerts and Musicale Regale fundraisers, and he worked at camp as the archery instructor. I already wrote that Joe was smart and did well in school, earning certifications in three different disciplines. He was a good-looking guy. (Ackerley men are good-looking guys!) There were wonderful times spent with Joe on camping trips—sitting around campfires, listening to ghost stories Joe would tell, and playing charades. We stayed awake on Rocky Point beaches until midnight on New Year's Eves to watch Joe's famous fireworks displays. Joe liked to take solo hikes into the foothills for overnight camping trips to be with God and nature. And Joe was always ready to lend a hand. Each December, he was eager to help bring the Christmas tree into the house, and he helped hitch up the trailer when we were getting ready for a trip.

There isn't a day that goes by that we don't grieve Joe's death. Joe will always be a part of us. We are fortunate to have had the blessings of Joe in our lives for just a month short of thirty-three years. We will forever remember his kindness, spirituality, intellect, humor, talent, quality of character, and love for God and his family. (*We love you, Joe. We miss you.*)

# 8

## Our Future Is Bright

Why does this chapter get a spot in my book? It is, after all, a visit to the future, and a memoir puts the spotlight on the past. My memoir has a special purpose, and that is to illustrate to people how they can be in a very *bad way*, and they don't have to stay there. The "bad way" can be temporary.

*The Lord told me to look straight ahead.*

I have a new job waiting for me. From now on, when people call me Doctor, I won't have to explain that I'm a nurse practitioner. I am a doctor of nursing practice! The Lord put me on this path long ago, and now I'm where he wants me to be. The biggest surprise for me now is that I am working alongside those professionals who cared for me years ago! God is amazing! My happiness is being in God's will. I'm working with people who are smart and kind, and I know I will continue to learn from them and use what I learn to be better at my work. I will provide even better service to those who are in my care tomorrow and tomorrow and tomorrow. That's just the way it goes.

Still, work is not my life. Julian and I will take our thirty-three-foot trailer to Vermont to be near to Jennifer's and Jesse's home. We'll take our trailer on camping trips. It provides us with a luxurious "shelter" … complete with a large TV. As a matter of fact, we may move ahead to purchase or rent a bus for long-term trips. *It's a safety thing.* We'll have to investigate this further. But one way or another, we intend to "hit the road." We'll return to many of the places we visited with our children when they were young: Yellowstone National Park, Mt. Rushmore, and Yosemite National Park. We covered the whole United States when the children were small. Julian returned to some of these places with the Boys Chorus, but I will be happy to see them again, and so will he. We have such a beautiful country! As I tell Julian, we're not going to retire; *we're going to re-fire!* I did not invent this concept; there are books and articles that discuss the virtues of being productive. We know that God wants to use us all the days of our lives.

When we're at home and I'm not so busy, I'll relax—practice my piano and guitar, and give myself more downtime, which is probably long overdue, especially in light of my battle with cancer and my age.

I definitely want to stop working as many hours as I do now, but I can continue to work with patients through TeleMed. As the name suggests, it is an electronic videoconferencing program. Someone employed at our clinic had to stay in Colorado to be with her ninety-year-old mother who needed her. She used TeleMed to work with her patients in Arizona even though she was far away. In short, TeleMed will enable me to extend patient care beyond the office. So while Julian and I travel, I can devote some hours to work, and in addition to the other benefits (e.g., using the medical knowhow I worked hard to acquire to help people), it will give us an income. Julian knows this is my intention, and he thinks it is a good idea. In order to expand my prescriptive privileges, I'll have to obtain licenses in more states. As of this writing, I have these privileges only in Arizona.

I just reconnected with my cousin after forty-seven years. I'd like to spend time getting to know him better. And this reminds me to be alert to similar opportunities. The more leisurely future opens up new possibilities.

From time to time, I know I'll awake at 3:00 a.m. to listen to new instructions from the Lord. I hear God with my soul. *He speaks through his Word in the Bible, and so things come to me as I'm think-*

*ing, reading.* God uses all kinds of messages to get to people. I'm ready to do his bidding. In addition to the "wake-up calls" (no pun intended), I pray, "Awesome God, awesome respect," each evening. This won't change.

## Seventy-Five Thousand Dollars and a Shield

I don't know what seventy-five thousand dollars refers to or why the thought of being a human shield for someone slips in and out of my thoughts, but both notions are strong. In time, I know that a snippet of information that doesn't make sense to me will make sense. I also have the feeling that I'm going to return to Israel. I told Julian, "I guess you're going with me," and he said, "Okay!" I like Julian's response! We'll keep things *light*; or—as the *boomers* say— we'll go with the flow.

## Mature Christian

Charles Stanley advises when you are confronted by trials and tribulations, don't ask, "Why me?" Ask, "What can I learn from this?" I have learned so much. I'm closer than ever to being a mature Christian. This means I am able to use so many of the biblical teachings in my daily life. The operating word here is *use*. With God's help, I have come a very long way.

I was nominated for the Golden Flame Awards. This is an annual award honoring members and staff who have demonstrated outstanding achievements above and beyond expectations during the previous year. Following the nomination, I was honored to win the Partners in Recovery Staff Award. The award is given to a staff person who embodies the principles of recovery in their work through advocacy, encouraging independence, and hope. This would never have been possible without God first and foremost in my life.

Just as Jesus took three of his disciples up to the mountaintop, as written in Mark 9:2-9, so he has taken me to heights never imagined. Stephen Curtis Chapman says it so well in one of my favorite songs "The Mountain." The words express faith strengthened by the experience of living life and having respite in God's care "Up on the Mountain."

No telling what God has in store next for his child. To borrow a few more words (and favorite songs) from Stephen Curtis Chapman, it is important to "Remember Your Chains." My prison chains are broken and gone, though I will never lose sight of how I was set free. My faith is secure in him, and it's his "Great Adventure" that I would not want to miss for anything!

# A Portion of Jane Ackerley's Curriculum Vitae

Here, in part, are the curriculum vitae I put together:

*Education*

> Doctor of Nursing Practice Degree
> > Texas Christian University, Ft. Worth, 2014
>
> Psych-Mental Health Nurse Practitioner Certification
> > University of Arizona, Tucson, 2007
>
> Master of Science Major: Psych-Mental Health Nursing
> > University of Arizona, Tucson, 1989
>
> Bachelor of Science Major: Nursing
> > University of Arizona, Tucson, 1981
>
> Associate Degree Major: Nursing
> > Pima Community College, Tucson, 1974

*Travel*

> Bahamas 2016
> Hawaii 2016
> Switzerland, France, Germany, Poland, 2015
> China, twenty-three cities, 2013
> China-Beijing, Singapore, Xin Zaho, 2011

South Korea, Japan, Hawaii, 2010
Russia, Kazakhstan, Czech Republic, 2008
Korea, Jeju, Hong Kong, July, 2007
United States of America, visited fifty states, 1974-2007
Mexico, 1970-2007
South Africa, March 2004
Germany, Czech Republic, Austria, July 2001
Thailand, Vietnam, China, South Korea, Taiwan, Hawaii, February and March 2001
Chili, Argentina, Uruguay, August 2000
China, Hong Kong, August 1999
Canada, February 1999
Spain, France, Italy, Germany, Belgium, Austria, Switzerland, England, June and July 1997
Spain, France, Italy, March 1996
Hawaii—Kauai, Maui, Oahu, 1995
Australia, New Zealand, 1993
Russia, Poland, Germany, Austria, February 1990
China, Hong Kong, Japan, Hawaii, March 1987

*Foreign Language Skills*

Advanced Spanish, Pima Community College, N. Davison, 2002
Advanced Spanish, Language Horizons, D. Castro, 2001
Intermediate Spanish, Language Horizons, D. Castro, 1999-2001
Beginning Spanish, The Bernard Language School, M. Rubiner, 1998-1999
Beginning Conversational Spanish, Pima Community College, N. Davison, 1997

*Educational and Professional Honors and Awards*

Winner of Golden Flame Partners in Recovery Staff Award, 2015

Recognized at the Harris College Academic Achievement Banquet for Outstanding Academic Work, April 2014

Kudos-Customer Service Nomination, May 2013

Nominated by peers for Excellence in Service Award, December 2011

Nominated by peers for Excellence in Service Award, December 2010

Nominated by peers for Excellence in Service Award, December 2009

Recognition by the Medical Director and Chief Executive Officer for outstanding patient care, February 2009

Kudos-Customer Service Nomination, November 26, 2008

Certificate of Achievement, for outstanding contributions in substance-abuse, general mental health, and prevention services, La Frontera Center

Recognition for Exceptional Nursing Services, national and international travel, Tucson Arizona Boys Chorus

Recognition for "A Teacher That Makes a Difference," selected for the National Honor Society Induction, Amphitheater High School

Employee of the Month, for contributions to the coordination/management of Infection Control, Charter Behavioral Health Systems

CCRN, successful completion of the national certifying exam for critical care RN

APPENDIX B

# Funeral Mass Program for Joseph Ackerley and Eulogies

Joseph Julian Ackerley
Funeral Mass Program
Monday, January 30, 2012
Our Mother of Sorrows Church
10:00 a.m.

Prelude Music
Entrance: "Rain Down" DD #134
First Reading: Wisdom 3:1-9 (C-3, p. 38)

Gene Ackerley
Responsorial: "The Lord Is My Shepherd," (R&A p. 112, sung)

Second Reading: Romans 6:3-9 (E-3, p. 59)
Gosp. Accl: "Alleluia" (sung)
Gospel: John 11:17-27 (G-14, p. 83)

Deacon Keating Ackerley
Off: "Be Not Afraid" SS #170
(Bread and wine plus symbols of Joseph's life will be brought to the altar by Jennifer, Jane, Julian, and pallbearers)

Holy: Mass of God's Promise
Mem. Accl: "Save Us, Savior of the World"
Great Amen: Mass of God's Promise
Our Father: Recited
Lamb of God: Mass of God's Promise
Com: "Shepherd Me, O God" SS #59
"He Is Exalted" SS # 179

Eulogy: Jennifer, Jane, and Julian Ackerley
Video of Joseph and his family
Rec: "River of Glory" SS#135

*Joseph Ackerley Funeral Mass*
*Eulogy Introduction, read by Julian Ackerley*

Thank you for being here. This wonderful turnout today and at the rosary and visitation last night is a loving testimony to the contributions Joseph made to the lives of many.

Jane, Jennifer, and I have been overwhelmed by the outpouring of support. We are sustained by beloved family, extraordinary friends, and by our faith.

We thank Msgr. Cahalane for his compassionate spiritual guidance and everyone here at OMOS, our friends at Brings, the St. Francis de Sales choirs, and all of you for making this a memorable occasion.

The purpose of our gathering is to praise God for Joseph's blessing in our lives; embrace our sadness; acknowledge our love; share thoughts, feelings, stories; and eat. Joseph would be interested in what there is to eat. Thanks to the MOSES group and others for providing the lunch refreshments after the service.

There is pain and sorrow to bear, but we all should be comforted by the warmth of our memories. Jennifer, Jane, and I will each share some brief thoughts about our beloved Joseph.

*Mom's Eulogy for Joseph, January 30, 2012*

Joseph was my hero, managing his illness every day to the best of his ability. If he had been afflicted with cancer, we could talk about it openly, but a problem with mental health is different. Joseph asked us not to talk about it, and so we respected his request for confidentiality. It was not until the last few years, as the progression of his illness became much worse, that we were given permission to discuss it.

As a psychiatric nurse practitioner, I know there is a stigma associated with mental illness. The stigma can only lead to discrimination and inaction. It is important that we challenge those stereotypes and educate people about the reality of mental illness. It is a physiological and biological disorder. Mental illness is a sick brain as diabetes is a sick pancreas or cardiovascular disease a sick heart. Premature infants are at greater risk for psychiatric disorders due to brain injuries. Joseph was born premature. Misunderstanding mental illness and lack of knowledge about psychiatric disorders will only continue to marginalize the people that need our acceptance and help.

Each year the National Alliance on Mental Illness, known as NAMI (N-A-M-I), encourages all of us to stamp out the stigma surrounding mental illness. Joe and I are "Stigma Stompers." NAMI organizes a walk annually to increase awareness of mental health issues. Last year over four thousand people participated in the 5-K walk. This year's event is happening on March 31.

Joe had so many wonderful attributes and was a gentle and sensitive person. He loved Jesus Christ with all his heart. I have to tell you that I am a little directionally challenged. I admit that I take "the scenic route" to get places more than I would like to admit. Joseph frequently led the way and helped me with directions. There is, however, one direction that we both know very well, and that is *true north*. And we know how to get there. There is only one way, and that is through Jesus Christ. The four Js—Joseph, Julian, Jennifer, and Jane—will be together again someday with our Lord and Savior Jesus Christ.

Joe and I rode bikes together, played guitars together, and rode around together in his goofy cars. I always told him he should write a book about all his car adventures. I especially like the one about the car that wouldn't go in reverse. We parked on University Avenue one day, heading straight into the parking space, and when we left, we had to open the front doors of the car and, on each side, stick our foot out and push on the ground to get the car to go backward. Of course, all the university students were sitting there at the sidewalk cafes, watching us. It was a good laugh.

Romans 8:28 says, "And we know that all things work together for good to those who love God and are called according to his purpose." Good things have already started to happen following Joe's passing. There has been healing, blessings, and forgiveness that might otherwise not have taken place *and* the opportunity to witness to all of you about Jesus Christ. Joe would have loved this.

We would like to thank La Frontera Arizona Behavioral Health Center for their compassionate and quality care during Joseph's illness. We will always be grateful for their concern and expertise.

I miss you, Joe. I love you, and I will see you again in God's perfect timing.

*Jennifer's Eulogy for Joseph, January 30, 2012*

I miss my brother immensely—more than words can say. Yes, Joe did suffer from mental illness, but he had many great days too. I love my brother with all my heart! He was always there for me during guy problems, school problems, car problems. Joe could fix anything.

I have many precious memories of Joe: being pulled in the wagon from his bike, coffee dates, Nintendo wars, him convincing me there was a UFO in our backyard. But one of my most recent memories is playing basketball with him when I came home in December. Our full basketball game turned into a half-court game, which quickly turned into a game of *horse*. We joked it should be a game of *cat*. We spent that entire day together. I remember hugging him and thinking how our time together was so precious. *He* is so precious.

Joe taught me two major things in life: first, Jesus Christ is our Lord God and Savior. Jesus's death washed all our sins clean. And to those who believe in him, which Joe and our family do, they will have eternal life. And, second, rap music can be fun!

I love you, Joe, and will keep you close to me as I journey on. I look forward to reuniting with you. I love you forever and always.

*Dad's Eulogy for Joseph, January 30, 2012*

Dearest Joseph,

You have been an enormous blessing in my life. I have so many wonderful recollections from the moment of your birth to the last phone conversation we had on the day you went home to God.

The joy of fatherhood is simply remarkable. You were born six weeks premature amidst great concern for your health and viability. Holding you for the first time when you opened your eyes and looked right at me was a father-son bond made at that moment that I will never forget. God was with us … and my life would never be the same.

As a child, you did amazing things every day. Just having you say, "Hi, Dad," was special to me. I always cherished the family time we had together on our vacations, camping trips, and special outings. But equally memorable were the everyday things, the daily routine, and the knowing you were close … not only physically but always in my heart and mind.

You consistently did well in school. I also remember how wonderful it was for you to be in the Boys Chorus. Those were some of the best years of my career because I had the opportunity to experience them with you. I loved having you as a chorister, traveling, singing, performing, roping, and being together. I fondly recall our four Boys Chorus tours, especially to Washington, DC, to sing at the White House for then president Bush and to Australia, New Zealand, and Hawaii.

I also cherished your Boys Chorus connection as an adult in the Alumni Chorus, you going to concerts and Musicale Regales and working at camp.

I remember your piano lessons and recitals, your legendary bike rides around the neighborhood and into the desert, and the bike jumps off your homemade ramps of plywood and bricks.

I remember your interest in everything mechanical, especially taking things apart learning how they work; your football at Salpointe, basketball in our backyard; and your love of your cars—the Volkswagens, the Celicas, the Civic, the Toyota Tacoma, the big Town Car, and the Maxima. I remember you bodysurfing in the Southern California waves, waterskiing on Lake Roosevelt, and riding ATV up Competition Hill in Rocky Point.

I remember wonderful times sitting around campfires, hearing your ghost stories, playing charades, and staying up on New Year's on Rocky Point beaches with your famous firework displays. I remember when you set off on your megaroad trips. You always loved to drive. I remember your Christian rap and continually admired your talent with words and rhyme; your bass playing and singing in the church choir; your solo hikes into the foothills for overnight camping trips to be with God and nature; your willingness to help out how you could, especially bringing the Christmas tree into the house and helping hitch the trailer on our trips.

I know how much you adore your family: Mom, me, Jennifer, Grandma and Grandpa Shinevar and all the

Shinevars, Grandma and Grandpa Ackerley and all the Ackerleys, cousins, aunts, and uncles. You have been an incredible son, brother, grandson, nephew, cousin, and friend.

Please know I was proud of you even through difficult times.

I want to remember the positives, your hugs, your excitement of seeing me, your smiles, and infectious laugh. I want to remember your sense of humor, your love of God and family, and the extraordinary love I experienced with the honor of being your father.

Joseph, I know the struggle of your illness. It was so difficult to see your pain, to know your anxiety, and to witness your battle. I was truly amazed how you carried on every day ... regardless of it being good or bad ... doing your absolute best.

Most importantly, I know your relationship with God and our Lord Jesus Christ. You were an inspiration. Your spirituality and desire to live your Christian faith is one of the most significant things I admired most about you. You were intentional about reading and studying scripture, constantly praying, sharing the gospel with others, and living your faith on a daily basis. I know your fondness of the Lord's Prayer ... a permanent reminder inscribed on the back of the gold cross you wore. The power of that prayer is also significant to me as we prayed it together in our last conversation.

I was reminded by a friend that all this is a part of God's overall plan. He knew when you were conceived. He knew your everyday joys and sadness. He knew your suffering, and he knew when he would call you home. We can never know the power of God's plan. We must put our faith in him.

I miss you, Joe. I love you, Joe. I hope you know the incredible depth of your father's love and admiration. May you be at peace in eternal rest. Watch over me, your mother, and Jennifer as we continue our human journeys until we all meet again in heavenly paradise.

With all my love,
Dad

# APPENDIX C

# A Mother's Day Song Joe Wrote

Joe wrote this note to accompany the rap music he wrote for me.

Dear Mother,
     This is a special song that I wrote for you. The lyrics are truly from my heart. Thank you for being such a wonderful person. You are indeed one of God's greatest gifts. I love you, Mom.

"My Mother"
By Joseph Julian

There is one person in my life
Who I dearly love
It is my mother, who means so much to me
She is a gift from above

There is one person in my life
Who I dearly love
It is my mother, who means so much to me
She is a gift from above
I love you, Mom!

I love you, Mom.

You are always there for me
I am always enthralled with your grace and sincerity
I am truly blessed to be called your son
The day you were born was the ultimate one.
For you are truly one of God's great creations
Your tender love and care is the ultimate sensation
Mother, your presence on this earth is a gift from above
To all the people close to you who can experience your love
Because your unconditional love runs deeper than the sea
I forever count myself worthy to be the child of thee
Your image is the likeness of the Blessed Virgin
And I pray for intercession on your behalf, to limit your burdens
You are special as a true disciple of Christ
Mom, you do it all for him and have a truly blessed life
That's why I write this song for you to commemorate
The fact that you are holy indeed, anyone should emulate
Your great gift of the spirit plus intelligence
And your relationship with Christ, bringing great reverence
This song's for you, I pray many blessings in store
Because you're like Christ
You are the one I adore

There is only one person in my life
Who I dearly love
It is my mother, who means so much to me
She is a gift from above

There is only one person in my life
Who I dearly love
It is my mother, who means so much to me
She is a gift from above

I love you, Mom!

Joseph wrote many cards to express his love. On December 13, 2011, he wrote,

Dear Mom,

Mom! Happy birthday to you! You are the greatest. May God *richly bless* you on this your special day. You are always there for me no matter what! I *love you* so much! Thank you so much for all you do for me and our family.

Love,

Joe

"And if I have all faith, so as to remove mountains, but have not love, I am nothing" (1 Corinthians 13:2). I have so much love for you, Mom!

Here is another letter from Joe to our family on February 14, 2001.

Dear Family,

HAPPY VALENTINE'S DAY!

This is a very special day for loved ones in our lives. That is why I am taking this opportunity to express how much I truly love each one of you. Thank you so much for all of the unconditional love and support!

Each one of you means so much to me, and I am so happy to have such beautiful souls like you in my life. What an inspiration you are all to me. I appreciate my loving, caring and spiritual family so much!

I love, from the bottom of my heart and soul, you: Jennifer, Mom and Dad! You are all so special to me and so loved! Happy Valentine's Day!

My Sincerest Love,

Joseph

# APPENDIX D

# Excerpts of Christian Rap Music Written by Joseph Ackerley

Joe was a prolific songwriter. These are just a few samplings of the many songs he wrote primarily for God. Joe wrote Christian rap. Here is part of two of his songs. When you read "Acksking" that is Joe's nickname he invented.

"Unworthy"
By Joseph Ackerley

I'll try to write this song, but it just seems so inadequate
To all the songs you wrote just for me, your lyrics are immaculate
You are immaculate, ever since your Holy Spirit conception
And you are approachable even in your ultimate perfection
And my method is what I have to give to you
I love you with all my heart and soul
You brought me through
The pains that were unbearable, you never let me go
I know now why you were breaking me to the lowest of the low
So I would completely abandon myself and you use me for your will
You made me a stronger person
It's great power you instilled
But I will never forget how you were always there for me
But I was so stubborn God, and that's why I needed breaking

I prolonged the procedure and delayed the undertaking
But through it all, I knew to always rely upon you
When my life was smashed up, rock bottom, it was you I called to
And you know what, whenever I did that, it worked
You always were there at my worthlessness, my worst
And that is just one of the thousands of reasons why I love you
I pledge my life to you and know that there is nothing above you
It's you, the majestic King of all creation, and my life
Thank you sincerely for the gift of your salvation
I love you, Jesus Christ, from the bottom of my soul
My heart overflows with love for you I do extol
My mind is on point with love for you at the forefront
And my strength of love is real, comparable to a fortress.
It's your love Acksking, trying everything I can do.
To dedicate all of my love, and my life just for you!
And here's this song too.


True love and life, Jesus the Christ. Mwwaaahhh

*Acksking Ode to Christ*
By Joseph Ackerley


It's Acksking and I am sure that you have heard it before
There's only one thing on this earth that I truly adore
It's the one being that I am planning on seeing
When he comes back, the chosen few he will be leading
Because Acksking is filled with so much love
And admiration to the one giving blessings from above
He is always there for me and wants me to do more, to glorify and
praise him and receive the treasures in store
For me, because he loves me more than words can describe, to tell
you that I understand his infinite love would be a lie
He is the only person in this world that can make me cry
Jesus Christ is my one true love

Now let me tell you why
He gives me so much, way more than I can tell you
I can write a song trying to convey the peace he's led me to
But it always comes up short because his love is infinite
He showers blessings on me to the point I can't even ponder it
Any love that I would have directed toward him
Jesus Christ's love is times infinity, a love I can't comprehend
Now I can try to return it but my efforts are so weak
I do love Christ in return, to my deepest heart I reach
I keep coming up short as merely a human being
And I understand the reason your love reigns supreme
You love me greater than anything in existence
I know your love is true, 'cause when I pray to you, I can feel it
And it's all because of my unbreakable faith in you
That's the reason you love me so much and give great blessing too
But the one reason why I know you love me more than anything
Is the simple fact that you died for me, on that cross on Calvary
The most solemn oath of love and it was a testament to me
Jesus Christ, you are the most supreme, and that is why I sing
Because you gave me the gift of life and a true love toward you
After your greatest sacrifice for me, what else could I do
Than to dedicate my life to you and give you the life that's mine.
Jesus Christ, I love you dearly, strength, heart, soul, and mind!

# APPENDIX E

# Excerpts from Letters to Me from Some of My Students and Patients

Dear Jane,

Thank you so much for four wonderful months I had with you. I learned so much as a student and as a human being. You are a beautiful person inside and out.

Dear Jane,

I want to thank you for so willingly having me as a student. You have made my transition into clinical year an easy and enjoyable one...you single-handedly filled me with self-confidence. I could not have asked for a better experience or a better preceptor.

Dear Jane,

Your kindness, patience and excellent rapport with your clients is something I hope to mimic in my future career in healthcare. It was such a pleasure working with you. I can only hope to be as good of a provider as you.

Dear Jane,

I feel very blessed to have had you as a preceptor. I find your patience, knowledge, and devotion to Christ to be very inspirational. I hope to emulate your empathy and spirit throughout my practice.

Jane,

Thanks so much for being a fantastic mentor. My time at La Frontera has been great and you played a large role in that positive learning experience…you are so sweet and have such a love and empathy for your patients that is rooted in your past experiences and in your faith. I know your patients can feel that genuine concern and have a deeper respect for you as their provider because of it.

And Excerpts from a Few Letters from My Patients

Dear Jane,

I would like to send you my deepest sympathy and condolences in the passing of your mother. May God give you the comfort and peace that you seek…Jane, I would also love to sincerely thank you so much for being so helpful to me all these years during my mental challenges. You are definitely an angel to me. I truly love the wonderfully amazing person you are.

Thanks for all you do and have done to get me in good mental health and state of mind. You are outstanding.

Dear Jane,

I am so glad you are my doctor, you are so nice and kind, please don't leave me. I have nine months clean and sober now and I need you.

# APPENDIX F

# Some of My Favorite Books, CDs, and DVDs

## Books You May Want to Read

*Doctrinal Bible Studies Catalogue* by R. B. Thieme, Jr., Bible Ministries, www.rbthieme.org (Note: R. B. Thieme Jr. explains, after salvation, how you move on in your Christian life to be a mature believer.)

*10 Ways to Execute Your Faith and How to Live Day by Day* by R. B. Thieme, Jr., Bible Ministries

*My Utmost for His Highest* by Oswald Chambers, 1992, Discovery House Publishers (Note: this is a powerful daily devotional of Chamber's classic book.)

*Hudson Taylor's Spiritual Secret* by Dr. and Mrs. Howard Taylor, 2009, Moody Publishers (Note: this is the story of a man who lived his life with complete abandon and dependence on God.)

*The Edge of the Divine: Where Possibility Meets God's Faithfulness* by Sandi Patty, 2010, Thomas Nelson, Inc. (Note: the acclaimed soprano tells of her journey from the brink of physical disaster to spiritual fulfillment.)

*The Prayer of Jabez: Breaking through to the Blessed Life* by Bruce Wilkinson, 2000, Multnomah Publishers (Note: discover how this remarkable prayer can release God's favor, power and protection.)

*The Prayer of Jabez for Women: Breaking through to the Blessed Life* by Darlene Wilkinson, 2002, Multnomah Publishers (Note: Reach for a life in which miracles happen. This book addresses the needs of women in today's world.)

*Experiencing God* by Henry T. Blackaby and Claude V. King, 1994, Broadman & Holman Publishers (Note: seek a more intimate relationship with your Creator, and experience the fullness of a life lived in fellowship with God.)

*God's Promises for You* by Max Lucado, 2005, www.hallmark. com (Note: an outline of God's many promises from the Bible)

*Into His Presence* by Charles Stanley, 2000, Thomas Nelson Publishers (Note: a year's worth of spiritual exploration)

*Breaking Free: Making Liberty in Christ a Reality in Life* by Beth Moore, 1999, Life Way Press (Note: a Bible study journey with you as the subject)

*Living the Extraordinary Life* by Charles Stanley, 2005, Thomas Nelson Publishers (Note: this is one of Joe's favorites)

*The Purpose Driven Life* by Rick Warren, 2002, Zondervan Publishers (Note: A number of my patients have read this book, and it has been life changing for them. I think it's worth bringing out a marching band to call this book to your attention! How's that for an endorsement?)

*The Hiding Place* by Corrie Ten Boom, 1974, Bantam Books

*The King James Version of the Bible*, Scofield/King James (Note: this version was recommended by R. B. Thieme.)

## Audio CDs (Some of My Favorites)

Point of Grace, "A Thousand Little Things"
Point of Grace, "Turn Up the Music"
Casting Crowns, "Thrive"
Casting Crowns, "Voice of Truth"
Casting Crowns, "Praise You in the Storm"

Bob Carlisle and other artists, "David: Ordinary Man … Extraordinary God"

World's Best: Praise and Worship Volume 3

Steven Curtis Chapman, "Heaven in the Real World"

Steven Curtis Chapman, "This Moment"

Steven Curtis Chapman, "Declaration"

For King and Country, "Crave"

Nichole Nordeman, "Woven and Spun"

WOW Hits 2004: 30 of the Year's Top Christian Artists and Hits

Crystal Lewis, "More Greatest Hits"

Twila Paris, "Greatest Hits"

Twila Paris, "He Is Exalted: Live Worship"

Jesus Christ Superstar, 1973

## DVDs (Some of My Favorites)

The Bible: The Epic Miniseries, 2013

Jesus of Nazareth, 1977

Prince of Egypt, 2002

Ben-Hur, 2016

## APPENDIX G

# A Few Words about Steven Curtis Chapman

Put the spotlight on Steven Curtis Chapman. This Christian singer performs for appreciative audiences everywhere. He is a songwriter, singer, record producer, actor, and author. If you don't know his name, you probably know his music. Artists like Sandi Patty, Glen Campbell, and Roger Whittaker have recorded his songs. He and his wife and family sustained the loss of a child too, when their adopted young daughter was accidently struck and killed by an automobile. Reportedly, Chapman is a devout Christian. I'm impressed by his achievements and his charitable nature. You may want to read more about him and will find lots of information on the Internet.

*"More" Section*

Websites that may be helpful:
National Alliance on Mental Health
NAMI, HelpLine 800-950-6264
3803 N. Fairfax Drive, Suite 100, Arlington, VA 22203
www.nami.org/About-NAMI

CDC Centers for Disease Control and Prevention
www.cdc.gov/Violence Prevention/suicide/Index.html.
There is a Suicide Prevention Lifeline at 1-800-273-8255

Rick Hughes Evangelistic Ministries, Inc. Cropwell, AL
800-831-0718 www.bigrick.org

R. B. Thieme Jr., Bible Ministries www.rbthieme.org

# Summary

God continues to teach me new things. I have been learning Bible doctrine from Charles Stanley for more than a decade, listening as I drove to work or taking notes during my lunch hours. While driving to church on Sundays, I discovered Rick Hughes on the radio. Of course God's timing is perfect, and the half hour it took to drive to church was the time the program was broadcast. From there, I was directed to R. B. Thieme Jr.'s Bible studies. Pastor Thieme uses the approach of exegesis, which is a critical interpretation of the original Hebrew and Greek scripture from the Bible. (I think of this as placing scripture in its historical context and not permitting the passage of time and changing points of view to camouflage the message.)

I learned how to stay in fellowship with God by using 1 John 1:9. As I maintain fellowship by naming my sins to God, I am able to build up my knowledge of doctrine on a daily basis by allowing God to continue to fill up my spirit. Then God is able to work through the Holy Spirit in my life. What a blessing that has been! I think I may have been allowing God to fill my spirit all along, but I was unaware of the mechanics of how to make it happen on a daily basis. I've learned that it's important to acquire these principles under a qualified pastor teacher who has studied the texts of the Bible from original words, context, and categories. This is how the truth is told. I just needed to be open to it. I have also learned that life is for the living. God gives us grace in living and in dying. Psalm 90:12 and Psalm 16:11 are just two verses about living life to the fullest.

I have come a long way during my lifetime. After "wandering the desert for forty years," I have found that the most important thing in life is having a relationship with Jesus Christ. This is what being a Christian is about. It's not about a religion but a relationship. I had a pretty low sense of self at times with lots of feelings of insecurity as I, with God's help, dug my way out from the bottom to reach the top. God has performed many miracles in my life, and from these, I have learned to care for others because others cared about me.

Today I continue to listen to Bible studies from R. B. Thieme Jr. on my MP3 player in my car. I get a daily dose of an hour or more as I drive to work and back. I present what I have learned to others when the opportunity arises and the person is willing to listen. It helps me to learn as I repeat the principles to someone else. I have found that the information is comforting to many of the clients that I serve in the mental health clinic. I will continue to pray and ask God to "use me up" and do his will in my life. Life and a relationship with Jesus are doing his will in serving others. I have a small replica on my desk of Jesus washing the feet of the disciples, which is a good reminder to me every day of what is most important. Of course, I reflect upon and write about my many blessings, my husband, my daughter, my son, our beautiful home, the people with whom I share my workday, numerous family members and dear friends. Early on in this book, I focused on misdeeds—a polite way of saying *sins*. No more. You have only to take notice of the title of this book, *A Place That's Warm and Beautiful*, to know that I am happy. *I am free. God is in control of my life.* That does not mean I will never sin, but I know how to recover quickly and stay on track.

How could I not tell you that no matter what challenges you're facing, you too can get to a better place? It's my hope that as you read these words, you can say, "I believe." Now you have only to act to get to your own *warm and beautiful place.*

*What seems to us as bitter trials are often blessings in disguise.*
                                              —*Oscar Wilde, actor, writer*

*One more thing …*

It has been a great pleasure to work with Jane. Her comments are typically laced with humor. She laughs easily even when I know she has had a long day of work with people who seek her out when they are in pain. She has every reason to feel weary and would probably enjoy a good meal, a hot bath, and time to sit down at the piano. For those readers who shall only meet Jane from afar (via this book and nothing more), I feel the pressing need to let them know that to work with her, to listen to her, to plan with her is a privilege. Assemble all the positive adjectives you can think of, and they apply to Jane. Here is the short list: authentic, compassionate, dedicated, hardworking, determined, devoted, and I shall stop now so we can get this book on its way to you!

Marilyn Pincus

Ackerleys 2000

Ackerleys 12-04

Ackerleys 1991

# About the Author

Jane Ackerley, DNP, MSN, APRN, PMHNP-C is a psychiatric nurse practitioner in Tucson, Arizona. She studied nursing at the University of Arizona and received her doctor of nursing practice degree from Texas Christian University. Dr. Ackerley practices at La Frontera Arizona and Carondelet Health Network St. Joseph's Hospital. She serves in the outpatient behavioral health community and inpatient drug and alcohol rehabilitation and mental health treatment.

Dr. Ackerley was the recipient of the Golden Flame Staff Award for Partners in Recovery at La Frontera and was recognized at Texas Christian University for Outstanding Academic Work. Ackerley's credentials as a psychiatric nurse practitioner are wide reaching. She has presented her evidence-based practice and theological views on suicide prevention and patient-centered care in various venues. Dr. Ackerley has extensive experience in working with indigent patients and the less advantaged.

Ackerley administers person-centered care in her practice. She has been recognized as a behavioral mental health professional who is not just knowledgeable, but listens well to her patients and offers a caring hand. Her unconditional regard of each individual, including them as a partner in the process, has been key in building a reputation of genuine concern for her patients.

Dr. Ackerley is married and has two children, is active in her church, and pursues other interests such as piano and guitar. She has had the opportunity to travel to thirty two countries over the past several decades for both professional and personal ventures.

CPSIA information can be obtained
at www.ICGtesting.com
Printed in the USA
BVHW04s1810040518
515201BV00002B/86/P